Hotel Warriors

*Prepared under the auspices of
the Media Studies Project,
the Woodrow Wilson International Center for Scholars*

Hotel Warriors
Covering the Gulf War

John J. Fialka

Foreword by Peter Braestrup

 Published by The Woodrow Wilson Center Press
Distributed by The Johns Hopkins University Press

Woodrow Wilson Center Special Studies

The Woodrow Wilson Center Press
Editorial Offices
370 L'Enfant Promenade, S.W., Suite 704
Washington, D.C. 20024-2518 U.S.A.
telephone 202-287-3000, ext. 218

Distributed by
The Johns Hopkins University Press
701 West 40th Street, Suite 275
Baltimore, Maryland 21211
order department telephone 1-800-537-5487

First published 1992

Printed in the United States of America

♾ Printed on acid-free paper

9 8 7 6 5 4 3 2

Library of Congress Cataloging-in-Publication Data

Fialka, John J.
  Hotel warriors : covering the Gulf War / John J. Fialka.
      p.   cm. — (Woodrow Wilson Center special studies)
  Includes index.
  ISBN 0-943875-40-4 : $9.75
  1. Persian Gulf War—Journalists. 2. War and the press—United
States. 3. Persian Gulf War, 1991—Personal narratives, American.
4. Fialka, John J. I. Title. II. Series.
DS79.739.F53 1992
956.704'3—dc20   92-7791
                                                                              CIP

Cover photographs courtesy of the U. S. Marine Corps
Cover design by Eddins, Madison & Spitz, Inc., Alexandria, Va.

Contents

Acknowledgments

The author wishes to thank Lawrence W. Lichty, Traci Nagle, and the rest of the staff at the Woodrow Wilson Center's Media Studies Project for the support that made this work possible. He also wants to express his gratitude to over a hundred fellow journalists who covered the war and shared their experiences for this study.

Foreword

Peter Braestrup

In this volume, the *Wall Street Journal*'s John Fialka has supplied us with the first detailed after-action report on the troubled media-military relationship during the Gulf War by a combat reporter who was there. As his narrative, based on interviews with colleagues and with the military, makes clear, he is not easy on either of the parties. He is particularly well-qualified to make such assessments. A widely respected military affairs correspondent, Mr. Fialka was one of the few to follow up the story of the 1983 U.S. invasion of Grenada, which initially had been closed to reporters, by finding out from military sources what really transpired. In the Gulf, during the allied buildup and the air campaign, he served for a time as a print pool coordinator (a thankless task), assigning colleagues to the journalistic teams, escorted by military public affairs officers, that visited American units in the desert. Once the 100-hour ground war began, he covered firsthand the rapid grueling advance of the Army's 3d Armored Division as part of Gen. H. Norman Schwarzkopf's end run around the western flank of Saddam Hussein's bomb-battered forces holding Kuwait.

John Fialka points out that the real test of the arrangements agreed to by the military and the press—censorship, pools, access, and military handling of communications and logis-

---

Peter Braestrup, a former correspondent for *Time*, the *New York Times*, and the *Washington Post*, is now Senior Editor and Director of Communications at the Library of Congress. He serves as Chairman of the Advisory Board of the Media Studies Project, Woodrow Wilson Center, and is the author of *Big Story*, an analysis of print and TV coverage during the Vietnam War, and other studies of wartime journalism.

tics—for the Gulf War came during the ground campaign, not during the prelude. Until Schwarzkopf's troops jumped off on February 24 (local time), the hundreds of newspeople in the hotels of Dhahran and Riyadh were roughly in the same situation as their journalistic forebears in London during the spring of 1944 who awaited the climactic D-Day landings by Gen. Dwight D. Eisenhower's Allied forces. Those World War II reporters attended briefings on heavy Allied bombing raids against targets in France and Germany, visited, under escort, U.S. units to do human interest features, submitted their dispatches to censorship, and chafed at the restrictions and lack of good stories and action pictures.

This parallel can be overdrawn: Eisenhower believed that the press had to be well accommodated, insofar as security permitted, to sustain public support at home. After two years of war, the military and the press were no longer strangers; in London, there were only 395 accredited newspeople, 180 American and 215 British, of whom 27 Americans were among those slated to accompany the D-Day landings; network television news did not yet exist, with its high costs, fierce ratings competition, and home office demands for dramatic footage; there was no 24-hour Cable News Network or C-Span, hungry for material to fill airtime, which permitted U.S. officialdom to present its case directly to the public at length every day without journalists as intermediaries. As they awaited D-Day, American reporters and their bosses in 1944, despite complaints over past Army fumbles and slow communications, were not fearful of deliberate media blackouts or simple fiascoes such as occurred during the 1980s in Grenada and Panama. (The U.S. invaded Panama in December 1989.)

There were media complaints right from the start of Operation Desert Shield/Desert Storm. For example, not quite a month after the Iraqis overran Kuwait and three weeks after George Bush dispatched the first American ground troops to Saudi Arabia, there came a bitter protest from Michael Gartner, president of NBC News. On the op-ed page of the *Wall Street Journal* (August 30, 1990), he wrote, "Here's something you should know about that war [sic] that's going on in the Gulf: much of the news that you read or hear or see is being censored. . . . There is no excuse for this kind of censorship [which] exceeds even the most stringent censorship of World War II." The press was shut out of Grenada, he wrote, "cooped up in Panama, and put on the late plane [carrying the Pentagon press pool] into Saudi Arabia." Once again, he concluded hyperbolically, the Pentagon had no use for the "facts."

What Mr. Fialka makes clear, as other postmortems often do not,[1] is that the Gulf War was a peculiar episode in the history of U.S. wartime media-military relations and in the evolution of modern journalism. As he suggests, memories of the Vietnam War helped shape attitudes in the Gulf. President Bush promised the public (and the Pentagon) that the effort against Iraq would not be ambiguous, contradictory, "another Vietnam." He called up the reserves, secured the assent of Congress and the support of the United Nations, defined the objective, fixed a decisive strategy, and was prepared to use maximum force. That the president would let the military run the battle was of great importance to Gen. Colin Powell, chairman of the Joint Chiefs, and to General Schwarzkopf. Unlike his counterparts in Vietnam, General Schwarzkopf would not be second-guessed daily by anxious civilians in Washington. What this meant, in effect, was that General Schwarzkopf decided how much command support to give to public affairs officers and upwards of 1,600 media representatives in Saudi Arabia;[2] Pete Williams, the articulate spokesman and assistant secretary of defense for public affairs, could arrange daily televised briefings in the Pentagon and listen to media complaints, but he could only negotiate with Central Command in Riyadh. And by all accounts, General Schwarzkopf, facing a host of imponderables, wanted maximum feasible control over all aspects of Desert Shield/Desert Storm, including media coverage to which he was extremely sensitive.

Reinforcing General Schwarzkopf's sensitivities was a hangover from Vietnam shared by many senior Army officers. The press was not to be trusted; biased journalism had, by itself, turned the American public against the Vietnam effort (a notion rebutted by much scholarly research); and, if given half a chance, newspeople, especially ratings-hungry television people, would portray the military in a bad light. (This was the mirror image of the Left's complaint—that the major media were de facto allies of the government.) Oddly enough, during the five months preceding the ground offensive, many prominent journalists also invoked the Vietnam experience—as a kind of a Golden Age. They did not recite the complaints of the 1960s about official "lies" and recurrent friction between reporters and officialdom. Rather, they called for a return in the Gulf to the military-press arrangements of the Vietnam conflict:

reporters in Vietnam agreed to follow certain rules and were allowed to hitchhike, often unescorted, to American units in the field. In contrast to the regime in World War II and Korea, there was no censorship of their dispatches.

What this appeal to Vietnam precedents ignored was history. Vietnam was a low-intensity conflict against a foe who, however tenacious and tactically adept, could not easily exploit (the few) inadvertent breaches of security. Moreover, except during the 1968 Tet offensive and a few other crises, the press put few burdens on U.S. military logistics or on unit commanders; seldom were more than 40 American journalists out in the field on a given day.

The Gulf exercise, as John Fialka notes, was something else. It was a Big League buildup, but combat did not begin for five months. Security was tight, and there was often tension between the press and the military in the field. Then the air campaign, inevitably, put the horde of journalists in Saudi Arabia at the mercy of the official briefers, as in England in 1944. (Schwarzkopf's briefers did not show video clips of smart bombs that missed their targets.) There was no room for journalists aboard most allied combat aircraft. Even a ride aboard the big B-52 bomber, sought by some journalists, would have yielded little except a view from 30,000 feet of dusty explosions in the desert. For the first time in U.S. military history, however, there were Western television journalists in the enemy capital— and vivid, if selective, film of the damage wrought by American firepower. To any alert American TV viewer, the air war did not look like a Nintendo game.

The ground offensive was conceived as a conventional set-piece attack employing surprise, fire, and maneuver. The foe seemed equipped to exploit any revelations. The distances were vast by Vietnam standards. The strain on communications and logistics across the desert was considerable, yet there was a plan to take more than 130 journalists in pools to units in the field. And there were hundreds of journalists, technicians, and support staff waiting to follow; many, perhaps most, were ill-prepared to describe or assess American performance on the battlefield, a problem already evident in the reporting at Grenada and Panama. With the end of the draft in 1972 and the influx of women into journalism, the culture gap between journalists and the U.S. military had widened greatly since Vietnam.[3] Increasingly, tactics, logistics, weaponry, and military language had become as foreign to most American reporters—

and their lower-echelon bosses—as the basics of American football were to, say, Kuwaitis. This became obvious early during the Gulf buildup. It did not increase confidence in the press among military commanders. Some editors contend that a good reporter can cover anything, but they do not send people to cover the Super Bowl who know nothing of the game. If, as some critics were later to claim, journalists were bamboozled by the military, many were as much victims of ignorance and their own short attention span as of manipulation.

The sins of the journalists do not excuse the sins of General Schwarzkopf's Central Command in failing to supply the necessary means and to insist that all Army field commanders make adequate provision for the press assigned to cover U.S. troops when the ground war began. The British did so, at least for television; the two U.S. Marine divisions, at the behest of the Marine Corps' commandant, Gen. A. M. Gray, did their best— and garnered far more than their proportionate share of coverage. Censorship was not the problem. As Mr. Fialka shows us, access and communications were what too many Army units failed to provide—and as a result, the public did not get a clear, timely picture of the crucial Army effort, an effort that revealed the troops, their equipment, and their commanders in the great test of combat.

That Americans, judging by the postwar polls, felt that neither they nor the news media were ill-served by the Gulf War arrangements is interesting but not conclusive; victory was swift and relatively painless. Both Washington policymakers and senior Army officers should not embrace the notion that handling the news media Gulf War–style is the way to do things next time. Nor should journalists be fixated on the Gulf experience. "Next time" will be different. Improved technology will make journalists less dependent on military communications, and censorship will be harder to impose. Access will still be vital. Logistics will be strained. Presumably, both the Pentagon and the news organizations will ponder alternatives to the high-cost, low-benefit horde journalism and long-lived heterogeneous media pools of the Gulf War. And there is talk of appropriate remedial training for journalists and the military.

Both sides will have to do some rethinking.

The basic point John Fialka makes is that the nation and the armed services are best served, as they have often been in the past, by competent firsthand reporting of military performance, good and bad. Despite its fits and fumbles, as a Twentieth Century Fund task force suggested after Grenada, "our free press, when it accompanies the nation's soldiers into battle, performs a unique role. It serves as eyewitness; it forges a bond between the citizen and the soldier and, at its best, it strives to avoid manipulation either by officials or by critics of the government through accurate independent reporting. It also provides one of the checks and balances that sustains the confidence of the American people in their political system and armed forces."[4]

Notes

[1]See Everette E. Dennis et al., *The Media at War: The Press and the Persian Gulf Conflict* (New York: Gannett Foundation, 1991); Jacqueline Sharkey, *Under Fire: U.S. Military Restrictions on the Media from Grenada to the Persian Gulf* (Washington, D.C.: Center for Public Integrity, 1992); *The Media and the Gulf: A Closer Look* (Berkeley: Graduate School of Journalism, University of California, 1991); Robert Wiener, *Live from Baghdad: Gathering News at Ground Zero* (New York: Doubleday, 1992); Theodore Draper, "The True History of the Gulf War," *New York Review of Books*, January 30, 1992, pp. 38ff.

"Operation Desert Shield/Desert Storm" in *Military Review* (September 1991) includes an essay on media-military relations by Maj. Gen. Winant Sidle, USA (ret.), former military public affairs chief in Vietnam and head of the Pentagon panel studying military-press relations in 1984 after Grenada. *Pentagon Rules on Media Access to the Persian Gulf War* (Washington, D.C.: Government Printing Office, 1991) is a valuable sourcebook put together by staffer Steven L. Katz for the Senate Committee on Government Affairs after its February 20, 1991, hearing.

[2]The peak number of media representatives present in Saudi Arabia for the Gulf War has been—and may always be—a matter of dispute. The 1,600 figure is an estimate based on the best available U.S. military records; the total includes not only reporters and camera operators, but also TV technicians, drivers, assistants, and sundry other support staff. One postwar investigation led by Hearst Washington Bureau Chief Chuck Lewis puts the peak number of true journalists—reporters, TV crew members, still photographers—at 600 (still a record for any U.S. war since 1945). However, some American—and many other foreign—journalists apparently did not register with U.S. or Saudi officials; indeed, the Saudis have claimed that as many as 5,000 foreign media people were in-country, and although they do admit some duplication errors, we find no documentation for such a high claim.

[3]Peter Braestrup, *Battle Lines: Report of the Twentieth Century Fund Task Force on the Military and the Media* (New York: Priority Press Publications, 1985), p. 9.

[4]Ibid., p. 13.

The Persian Gulf Region

From The Media at War: The Press and the Persian Gulf Conflict. *Copyright 1991 by the Freedom Forum Media Studies Center. Reprinted by permission.*

Chapter 1

The Business of Covering a War

"Good Morning America" (ABC) broadcasts live from Saudi Arabia during the week of November 19–23, 1990. (U.S. Marine Corps Photographic Division)

In mid-February 1991, as winter rains began to produce a thin green stubble of grass in the barren, rock-strewn deserts of northern Saudi Arabia, the processing began in Dhahran to move the last group of journalists who were going north to cover combat units now poised to strike Iraqi forces.

For most of us who had never covered a war before, it was the beginning of a brief, violent, and very strange adventure: an uneasy marriage of green reporters and an untried all-volunteer army of soldiers, most of whom had never been under enemy fire.

Much of what we wrote and videotaped out there remains unread and unseen to this day because the "100-Hour War" was presented to most viewers and readers in a tidy, antiseptic package. It was a finely orchestrated burst of high-tech violence where smart bombs landed precisely on the cross hairs; where generals made Babe Ruth style predictions that came true in real

1

time; where the "news" and its accompanying imagery were canned, wrapped, and delivered before the shooting was over.

It was a war that the great majority of journalists saw from the vantage point of the briefing rooms of posh hotels in Riyadh or Dhahran or from the gray metal chairs in the broadcasting studio on the E-Ring of the Pentagon. The "truth" for most news consumers during the war came from Pentagon-produced videotapes or on the fancy charts prepared to explain each bite-size chunk of the war.

For us it was different. We saw and experienced things that never made the briefings. We saw an Army public affairs system fashioned as a dead-end career for officers and staffed with a sprinkling of incompetents put there by media-wary generals, some of whom still blame the media for losing the Vietnam War. We saw the Marines and wrote too much about them because they had a flair for public relations that made some of us wonder whether they came from the same country that produced the Army. We were escorted away from most of the violence because the bodies of the dead chopped up by artillery, pulverized by B-52 raids, or lacerated by friendly fire don't play well, politically.

And we had a good, hard look at each other. Preparing the news is like making sausage: it is not necessarily a handsome process in the best conditions. But we found we had helped make a pool system that was geared for multiple failures. We had created rules that impeded coverage, and some of us were more intent on beggaring our competition than on participating in the creation of a large mosaic of reportage that was needed to make sense of this war as it swiftly unfolded. We were pack journalism forced into a girdle. When it came undone, so did we.

Only a very few of us managed to overcome all of this and produce stories that will live in history. Most memorably there was CBS's David Green with his television crew, floating out there on the very front edge of combat like a surfer balancing on the tip of an enormously powerful wave. They were in Kuwait City long before the allied liberators came.

And there were a lot of other stories you will never know because there are more of us who can relate to the experience of Scott Applewhite, an enterprising Associated Press photographer, who was the first journalist to arrive at the single most costly event of the war for U.S. forces—the crash of an Iraqi Scud missile into a barracks in Dhahran where 27 GIs were killed. For his pains, he was shoved around by guards, he had his film confiscated, and then he was escorted back to the Dhahran International Hotel by a public affairs officer. He was told "host-nation sensibilities" forbade any pictures. It was a convenient lie of a sort that may be part of the nature of modern expeditionary wars.

This is a brief synopsis of what we did and what we saw and a kind of quick tour for the general reader into the labyrinth where the press and the Pentagon are pinned down in a kind of static battle to see how the next war will be covered. It is not a trivial matter because wars and how they are perceived affect us all.

February 1991 was a long way from the inferno that greeted us when we first landed at Dhahran's sprawling airport in the panic of August 1990. Then there were heat waves dancing on the baking concrete as we passed rumors of Saddam's imminent invasion of Saudi Arabia. There was little to stop Iraq's armada of tanks between the Kuwait border and our blue, flag-festooned sanctuary, the Dhahran International Hotel, a posh, five-star establishment where the help was trained to smile and always remember our names. Every war produces a favorite hotel, and this one was right in the middle of the airport where U.S. troops were flowing in 24 hours a day. The soldiers were quickly marshaled from the C-5As and C-141s into dusty school buses that took them to their rough camps in the desert.

But we and our military handlers settled into the Dhahran International, where we spent many nights arguing how this war would be covered. There had been many false starts, but now in February, as a cool dampness permeated the desert outside, it seemed as though all the details were falling into place. We were ushered through a hotel storeroom where most of the equipment we would need was grabbed from an untidy stack of boxes: flak jackets, sleeping bags, charcoal-impregnated chemical warfare suits, rubber boots, gas masks, Kevlar helmets, and a special kit that had spring-loaded syringes filled with a chemical designed to block the effects of nerve gas.

A small army of technicians worked around the clock on the details. They provided the things that would be vital for civilians entering the battlefield: prescription lenses for the near-sighted gas mask wearer; a Geneva Convention badge that entitled the bearer to be treated as a noncombatant should he or she become a prisoner of war; a metal dog tag that would help the medics and chaplains do further processing on the battlefield. Mine said: "O Positive, Catholic."

The surge of new reporters, photographers, and radio and television people going north had all the herky-jerky of a last-minute decision, which it was. But behind it lay more than a half-year's worth of haggling between the Pentagon and media chieftains in Washington during the so-called warm-up period between Iraq's August 2d invasion of Kuwait and the allied air attacks that opened the Gulf War on January 17. In theory, there had been plenty of time for the policy governing the details of combat coverage to be worked out.

In fact there was no coherent policy. The widening chasm between American journalists and the military that was created during the Vietnam War remained largely unbridged. Nevertheless, most of us behaved as though we knew what we were getting into.

Everybody seemed prepared. The military had digested stacks of lessons-learned reports from seven years of experimentation with combat pools since the Reagan administration's much criticized, blacked-out invasion of Grenada in 1983. A team of no fewer than eight colonels who had worked on the reports was flown to Dhahran by the Pentagon to bless the new pool system that was now taking its final shape.

And the media had invested many millions of dollars in preparations for this moment. The hotel, long since booked solid by journalists, fairly bristled with sophisticated gear: laptop computers, satellite telephones, shortwave radios, fax machines, infrared cameras, and other electronic paraphernalia designed for nearly instantaneous communication from the desert. Months of arguing, pleading, back-stabbing, and screaming had taken place among the journalists in the hotel to allocate the combat slots that were now being filled.

We were not just going to write history; we were about to make history. Only 27 reporters had been allowed to land on the Normandy beaches with Allied troops on June 6, 1944. It is estimated that no more than 70 reporters were ever at the front at any one time during the Korean War. Of the 400 reporters accredited during the height of the Vietnam War, only between 30 and 40 could be found with combat units on a given day.

When we reached the desert, however, there would be 159 journalists covering U.S. units in the Gulf War, more than twice the combat coverage of any previous modern war. Was this a rosy moment in military-media relations? Hardly. We were an indigestible lump being fed into a military press-handling system that was woefully short of resources and teetering on the verge of collapse. The Pentagon had insisted that in this war reporters must be accompanied by military escorts, but it had not provided enough seasoned public affairs escorts and vehicles to do the job.

Worst of all we faced a jury-rigged system to get our copy, film, audio, and videotapes back. Civil War reporters, using the new high technology of the telegraph, were able to send reports of the Battle of Bull Run to New York in 24 hours.

In this lightning war, more often than not, technology stopped at the edge of the battlefield. Accounts of major battles took three to four days to reach New York because of a haphazard military courier system aptly dubbed the "pony express." One reporter's copy took as long as two weeks to make the eight-hour drive from the battlefield to Dhahran. A news photographer's film took 36 days. A television correspondent's videotape of two stories never got back at all.

If journalism is the first cut at history, ours was a poor attempt, despite the potential of unprecedented coverage we represented. Those who have taken the time to study our record have found large gaps in reportage—major battles that went virtually unrecorded, vital pictures that aren't there, a great deal of copy and videotaped footage that went no further than the editing room floor because it was outdated or not compelling enough to move editors.

The most detailed coverage of this war is contained in 1,352 field reports from newspaper, magazine, and wire service reporters. Assembled in bound notebooks, they nearly fill a four-foot library shelf. "I've read all of the pool reports," says Rick Atkinson, a *Washington Post* reporter now writing a history of the Gulf War. "It's often depressing simply because the quality of the pool reports is not very good. For my purposes, about one in 10 has anything in it that's useful. . . . It's really pretty superficial stuff."

"It was what we didn't get that bothers me," says Donald Mell, a photo editor for the Associated Press, who reviewed the thousands and thousands of pictures taken by over 40 photographers on the battlefield. "There were no dead Iraqi soldiers. We had these massive tank battles, but I did not see a picture of an American tank being fired during the whole thing."

Military censorship, in the literal sense of the word, was not the problem. Only five reports, 0.03 percent of those filed during and before the war, were sent to Washington for final review. Of those, only one was changed, according to the Pentagon.

"I guess you could call it censorship by lack of access," says Walter Porges, an ABC network vice president who has reviewed the pooled television coverage of the war. "There were a couple of big battles that nobody's seen any pictures of yet."

The networks' archives are bulging with videotapes that only the editors saw, after days of delay coming in from the field. Shortly after the war, according to Peter Van Sant, a CBS correspondent in London, his network seriously considered showing some of it in a week-long series entitled "The Unseen War." The idea was dropped, however, because two days after the war there were not enough combat correspondents left in Saudi Arabia to put the program together.

It was the same on radio. "Most of it [tapes from the battle-field] came in after the war and a lot of the stuff that came in after the war never got used," says John T. Lyons, general manager of news operations for ABC radio who also coordinated the networks in the radio pool in Dhahran.

Contributing to the chaos was a competitive frenzy among editors to get on to the next story: the liberation of Kuwait City. The ground war ended at 8 A.M., Saudi time, on February 28. It was only then that most field commanders and combat troops were becoming free to talk about their exploits, but by then, reporters were rapidly vanishing from the battlefield. They were rushing in droves to Kuwait City.

Never mind that the freeing of Kuwait City was a largely symbolic event and that the experiences of the war are likely to fuel U.S. policy debates—especially budget debates—for years to come, the rush for news was driven in this war, as in no other, by the short attention span of television and its insatiable appetite for symbolic visuals. Thus, the people who fought the war found little in the way of an audience interested in hearing their stories.

It was bad enough that the public received a truncated, gap-filled picture from our efforts, but the result was actually worse than that: The picture that did emerge was distorted by the vast difference in skill and effort applied to the press relations job by the Army and the Marine Corps. If the PR rivalry between the two services involved in the ground war had been a basketball game, the score would have been Marines 149, Army 10.

This imbalance made it a much more dangerous game for ambitious reporters because so much was riding on the luck of the draw. If Ernie Pyle, the talented word-portrait painter of life in the foxholes during World War II, had managed to get in a Gulf War Marine pool, he would have risked being mobbed by officers vying to get him to cover their units. If he had been assigned an Army pool, however, he would have found a substantial risk of: (1) getting lost, (2) becoming unable to communicate, or (3) being ejected or isolated by Vietnam-addled field commanders who worried that journalists might get too close to their troops. For those of us who covered Army combat units in this war, it was often a combination of all three.

With the benefit of hindsight—which none of us carried in our bulky rucksacks—the biggest mistake we made was to skew the coverage in favor of the Marines. The main effort of the war was the Army's ambitious and historic flanking attack that looped up into the Iraqi desert, turned east, and smashed through Saddam Hussein's elite Republican Guard. The move made any coherent Iraqi defense of Kuwait impossible.

There were 295,000 Army troops in that effort and only 80,000 Marines. The Marines were moving directly north toward Kuwait City or waiting offshore in amphibious assault ships that never landed. The Marines fought some interesting battles, but their part in this war was never meant to be more than a sideshow. "They [the Army] were the main attack. We were the support," explains the Marines' field commander, Lt. Gen. Walter E. Boomer. "Our attack was to support it [the Army's mission], to tie up forces in southern Kuwait so they couldn't shift over to the main battle."

Yet for a variety of reasons—some having to do with the Army's much weaker grasp of PR, some having to do with logistical delays in filing stories—much of the press coverage during the war focused on the Marines, leaving readers and viewers unaware of the larger picture taking shape on the battlefield.

A detailed examination of the coverage of the ground war as reported in the nation's four largest newspapers and shown on its four television networks reveals that incidents involving Marines were mentioned 293 times by these outlets, as opposed to 271 mentions of the Army's activities. Viewers flipping channels or comparing newspapers would have been further confused over which military branch had the major role in this war.

For example, coverage of the Marines dominated the *Washington Post* (75 Marine incidents versus 61 for the Army) and the *Los Angeles Times* (62 Marine incidents versus 41 for the Army).

On the tube, ABC tended to focus nearly twice as much on Marine coverage (37 incidents versus 19 for the Army) and CBS reportage tended to follow in the same direction (30 Marine incidents versus 22 for the Army). The *New York Times*, *Wall Street Journal*, CNN, and NBC, on the other hand, all had more incidents involving Army units.

There were also major differences in the quality of reportage on the two services. Typically Marine battles were reported in detail, usually identifying the individual units involved. Army coverage, on the other hand, was often only briefly alluded to, and units were frequently referred to simply as being in the "VII Corps" or part of "allied armor units."

(To facilitate the bean counting here, an "incident" is defined as the description of a specific event in the ground war, either reported or depicted. The evening news shows of ABC, NBC, and CBS were compared with a 10 P.M. EST recap of each day's events run during the war on CNN.)

The final contribution to this shortchanging of the American news consumer came from the media itself. Although journalists love to reprint the cliché that generals are always preparing to fight the last war, this time the generals were ready for a new kind of war. Fast-moving maneuver warfare has been part of Army and Marine fighting doctrine for almost a decade.

It was the media that came mentally prepared to cover another Vietnam, where reporters could shift, unescorted, from unit to unit as the action dictated. Most of us were not prepared for a war of total, rapid movement over a dynamic, trackless, extremely dangerous battlefield where someone without tactical vehicles, navigation equipment, military radios, and protection could easily get lost or killed. This war was short, brutal, and effective, and it afforded most journalists no time to shop around.

If maneuver warfare is the model for wars of the future—and most generals believe it is—the media have some difficult questions to consider, beginning with the matter of how to control large numbers of journalists covering the battlefield. At some point, the numbers of journalists, as they did in this war, overwhelm the military's capabilities to accommodate them. The issue was ignored in Saudi Arabia where members of the pools and their organizations finally lobbied the Pentagon to double the slots in combat pools—a move that probably helped collapse the system, such as it was, for getting stories and pictures in from the battlefield.

Instead of throwing more money and journalistic troops at the problem, editors in Washington and New York will have to develop common strategies to cope with the realities of future combat. The prime question is, as one British editor put it, "if you have a man out on the battlefield with no means to report back, why is he out there?"

Left to their own devices, journalists in Dhahran tried to solve the numbers problem with a variety of political formulas, none of which seemed to serve the news consumer very well. It often included the creation of cartels within pools, cliques used by larger organizations to constrict coverage of smaller competitors. In the case of the newspaper pool, the leaders oscillated from a cartel to a one-person–one-vote rule that barred more experienced reporters from larger papers from working on the battlefield and flooded it with people from smaller outlets, many with little or no knowledge of the military.

As bureau chiefs back in Washington, who helped establish many of the pool rules, were making proud speeches about the First Amendment or romanticizing over the need for unfettered, unilateral coverage, the frustrating press battles in Dhahran over how to interpret their rules went on night after night. Fundamental questions such as, "What is a newsmagazine?" or "What constitutes a wire service?" reverberated, unanswered, through the halls of the hotel.

Meanwhile, the commanders were already quietly violating the most fundamental rule of coverage: that editors, not generals, pick the reporters who cover the war. In at least three cases, the generals simply ignored the rules, inviting favorite reporters with them and granting them communications priority to cover the war.

Reporters and photographers operating independently, the so-called unilaterals who were violating pool rules by going unescorted within 100 miles of the battle area, did fill some of the many gaps that resulted. They provided the first news of the prewar battle of Khafji and of the liberation of Kuwait City, where unilaterals beat the pool by an entire day. But unilaterals, under constant harassment by the U.S. military and sometimes under fire by the Iraqis, took enormous risks just to operate on the fringes of the war. For the most part, however, they weren't in a position to answer the biggest question that confronted Americans during the ground war: What was happening on the battlefield?

British viewers and readers, on the other hand, often knew more about their troops, and sooner. The British media, which had much less in the way of resources to put into the coverage of the Gulf War, invested reporters more wisely. While much of the American press's electronic equipment was left behind in Dhahran at the request of the military, the British army helped their press set up and use satellite phones and satellite broadcasting equipment in the battlefield.

"We did not miss deadlines," said one account in a report prepared after the war by the British International Press Institute.[1] "It was a good, principled relationship in which we had to reach accommodation under pressurized conditions without compromising the basic functions of either journalism or army operations."

With the exception of portions of the U.S. Marines' sector of the battlefield, no one could say that about the American effort. We all thought we had what we wanted, but few of us appreciated the difficulties of covering a war such as this. One U.S. television reporter had a prophetic vision as our truck bumped over the desert to the Army's section of the front. "We are like the proverbial dog that chases cars," he exclaimed. "Finally we caught one. Now what are we going to do with it?"

Note

[1]Peter Preston, comp., *Reporting the War: A Collection of Experiences and Reflections on the Gulf* (London: British Executive of the International Press Institute, 1991).

Chapter 2

The Army: "Business as Usual"

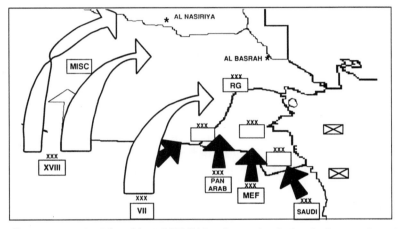

Troop movements of the celebrated "Hail Mary" operation during the first two days of the ground war, February 24–25, 1991. (U.S. Army)

Within hours of the launching of the largest military attack since World War II, the Army's system for supporting the reporters who were covering it collapsed. Only small pieces of it survived to help journalists with units in the battlefield during the 100 hours of the ground war.

Four U.S. divisions in the Army's VII Corps (the 1st and 3d Armored Divisions, the 1st Infantry Division, and the 1st Cavalry Division) were the spearhead of the attack. They included over 100,000 soldiers moving 100 miles northeast into the Iraqi desert and then cutting due east to shoot their way through the surprised remains of Iraq's tank-heavy, elite Republican Guard divisions.

11

The Army provided the crucial finale of the war. It was the Army's moment to shine after all the back-breaking work of moving the nucleus of VII Corps—the most heavily armored unit in the U.S. arsenal—from Germany in just under three months. It carried 32 reporters into battle with it.

But coverage problems had multiplied as the battle moved. There were no satellite phones out in the field for reporters to use. Neither Army field phones nor their tactical fax machines could be adapted to the Saudi's commercial phone system and most were off-limits to the press. The Army-designed pony express system of couriers and its teams of reporter escorts were hopelessly understaffed, underequipped, and poorly trained and motivated for the job. The upshot: As the battles raged, we (couriers, escorts, journalists) and news copy, film, and videotapes spent a lot of valuable time lost in the desert.

As line after line of Iraqi troops quickly folded under the shock of the heavy, rapid assault, the stage was set for one of the best U.S. Army stories ever. The embargo imposed by U.S. commanders on news of the gigantic troop movement had been lifted. The American public, even the Army brass in Washington, tired of hearing about the Marines, were frantic for news about the troops. But where there might have been a flood of news about the Army, only a trickle ever materialized. The Army had drifted into a black hole of its own making.

And it took heroic efforts just to generate that trickle. While most of us were lost or out of contact, Philip Shenon of the *New York Times* and Neil MacFarquhar of the Associated Press had flown over the horizon-to-horizon columns of the VII Corps in a military helicopter and had been briefed on its significance and its mission. It was Tuesday evening, February 26, the eve of the biggest tank battles of the war, and they were within a two-hour drive of pay telephones in Hafar al Batin, a Saudi crossroads town of storefronts and seedy hotels near the Iraqi border.

Their first obstacle was Maj. David Cook, 37, the tall, narrow-faced assistant public affairs officer of the corps. He wouldn't let them out of VII Corps's rear encampment area in the northern Saudi desert because the colonel commanding the base had given an order: There would be no trips to Hafar al Batin after dark because of a "terrorist threat."

Mr. MacFarquhar has vivid memories of the argument that followed. "We said that was ridiculous. We wanted to talk to the colonel who was head of the camp, but Cook wouldn't let us. There were public affairs officers there willing to drive us into town."

He remembers Major Cook sitting in his trailer/office placidly munching from a can of Corn Nuts and issuing orders about who was in charge of the detail that night to burn the human excrement at the latrine used by the 26 members of his public affairs detachment. The two reporters lost their tempers and began screaming at Major Cook.

Screaming at Major Cook rarely accomplished anything, although many journalists tried it. The press office of VII Corps had its own plodding rhythm. There was the *Jayhawk*, the corps's newspaper, to get out. There was the continuing dialogue about whether the soldiers from the Kentucky and Tennessee National Guard detachments would do the donkey work or whether Cook's people would do it. Those were problems Major Cook could deal with: It was the guardsmen who would burn the shit. But as far as getting two reporters with a world-class story to a phone, that seemed beyond him.

"If you had walked into that office," Mr. MacFarquhar recalls, "you would have never known that there was a major snafu out there about getting the copy back. If you asked them, they'd say everything is moving too fast and there's nothing we could do about it."

After enduring more screaming, Major Cook decided that there was something he could do. There was a small military airport, Al-Quysumah, within a 20-minute drive. The corps's drivers would help the reporters find a phone there.

Their next obstacle was their driver: Lt. Max Blumenfeld of the Tennessee National Guard. He seemed to hate reporters. "On the drive over there it just started spilling out, apropos of nothing," recalls Mr. MacFarquhar. "He said, 'You yelled at a commissioned officer. You guys are just a bunch of yuppies. You think you own the world.'"

There were seven people lined up in front of the single pay phone at the airport and, while the two reporters were trying to make sense out of their notebooks in preparation for the call, Lieutenant Blumenfeld was ushering other people into the line ahead of them. "He'd say 'Go ahead,'" recalls Mr. MacFarquhar, "'You're military. These people are just reporters.'"

When Mr. Shenon finally reached the phone, he realized he didn't have enough Saudi coins to complete the call. After borrowing some, he stepped back to the phone, prompting another outburst from Lieutenant Blumenfeld, who insisted that he move back farther in the line because five more soldiers had appeared to make calls to home. "You stepped in front of a commissioned military officer!"

It was well after midnight by then. East Coast morning paper deadlines were fast approaching. Lieutenant Blumenfeld then decided that the reporters had been so rude and uncooperative that they should be taken directly back to the base. There, luckily, using a makeshift connection through the military telephones, Mr. Shenon managed to get through to Dhahran. The result, after much clicking and broken phone connections, was the only news story to make it out of the VII Corps in the midst of its historic mission.

Lieutenant Blumenfeld, 32, went on to harass members of a newly arrived CNN television crew. According to Chris Turner, the crew's soundman, Lieutenant Blumenfeld was reluctant to take the crew to combat units. When he did, the lieutenant sometimes lobbied the unit's commander to make the reporters leave. "He [Lieutenant Blumenfeld] got us lost about five times, once in a mine field. It was a puckering experience," recalls Mr. Turner.

Lieutenant Blumenfeld, who has since been promoted to captain, says that while he doesn't necessarily hate the press, he does think that "the American media, from my point of view, cannot be cooperative. They are still out to, you know, let's get that scoop, let's make a name for ourselves, let's be the first one in." He denies asking commanders to order the CNN crew to leave, but he says some commanders wanted the reporters to go away for "security and safety" reasons.

Journalists elsewhere in the sprawling Army convoys did better. Some of the reporters in the 18th Airborne Corps, to the north and west of us, were getting stories out via a military fax machine. But the 18th wasn't running into much opposition. The story was the impending collision between the VII Corps and the Republican Guard. And most of us moving into battle formations with VII Corps may as well have been on the dark side of the moon. We never saw a courier during the entire five days of the ground war (or afterward).

The idea behind the pool concept, as it was hammered out in the Pentagon and in meetings with Washington bureau chiefs, was that reporters would be assigned to different units where they would be accompanied by an assigned military escort charged with assuring their personal safety and making sure their copy got back to the rear.

The journalists dotted all over the battlefield would file frequent reports, ideally generating "a mosaic," according to Col. William Mulvey. As director of the military's Joint Information Bureau (JIB) in Dhahran, Colonel Mulvey, 46, a soft-spoken West Pointer who led a rifle platoon in Vietnam, was the intermediary between the commanders out in the field and the press hordes in Dhahran.

His job was to be a kind of giant shock absorber. Journalists struggling to get out in the field screamed at him, lobbied him, and charmed him, and one, R. W. Apple of the *New York Times*, even threatened his job. At the same time, Colonel Mulvey had to cater to the whims of field commanders, all of whom outranked him.

The generals in the field controlled the assets, the jeeps, helicopters, public affairs officers, and the lines of communications, such as they were, and access to the units. All Colonel Mulvey and his staff in Dhahran could do was provide the reporters and suggest that units accept them. He had no trouble at all with the Marines, who had doubled their quota of journalists and were begging for more. "I saw that as an opportunity. I wish we had some Army general that had been asking 'would you send me some more,'" Colonel Mulvey explains.

Under pressure from the bureau chiefs in Washington and backed up by the Pentagon, Colonel Mulvey finally managed to raise the number of reporters in the field from 100 to 192 in the final hours before the ground war started on Sunday, February 24. After that, however, nothing seemed to work right. Now, as the nation's concern for the troops was reaching its peak, large pieces of Colonel Mulvey's mosaic had gone dark.

"I think we overwhelmed the system," says Lt. Col. James W. Gleisberg, the chief public affairs officer for the VII Corps and Major Cook's boss. In early January, he says he was told to get enough jeeps, escorts, and other provisions to accommodate seven reporters. He wound up with over four times that many, forcing him to put reporters at brigade level. "People at brigade level had never lived with media day in and day out before."

Lieutenant Colonel Gleisberg authorized a system whereby couriers from the brigades would take copy, film, and videotape to division headquarters. Each division had two couriers and two jeeps to last the entire war. When they left with copy they wouldn't return. They would take it back to the corps's rear base and from there couriers would drive it to King Khalid Military City where an Air Force C-130, the only aircraft the

Army's public affairs apparatus could get, flew the news cargo to Dhahran once a day, leaving at 7 P.M.

"Nothing moved at night because nobody knew the routes," he explains. At best, he says, the pony express took 72 hours to reach Dhahran. Other Army units, using the same system, weren't much faster.

Lieutenant Colonel Gleisberg, who was rarely seen by reporters, delegated the job of setting up the pony express to Major Cook, who assigned it to Capt. John R. Koko, a Kentucky National Guardsman who couldn't believe the Army was seriously considering it. "I was given a set of guidelines that no one in the civilian world could operate under," recalls Mr. Koko, who in private life is a vice-president of a Louisville health insurance company. "I was given no equipment and no explanation why."

Captain Koko suggested replacing the courier system with the Army's tactical fax machines, using them at night, when military traffic slowed down, but Major Cook rejected the idea because "the news was low priority." At least a day of delay was built into the ground courier system, Captain Koko believes, so that Major Cook could censor the copy, which he did. This was an additional level of review that was not authorized under pool guidelines, which only required reviews of copy in the field and at the Joint Information Bureau in Dhahran, but VII Corps did it anyway.

Captain Koko, who went to great lengths to help reporters in his role as an escort, had no public affairs experience. After the war he was given a poor rating by Major Cook for having a "bad attitude." Mr. Koko then resigned his Army commission. "Afterwards I heard from the Army that the pool system worked great. That's really scary to me," says Mr. Koko. "I felt that what they really wanted was public relations. Somebody writes something negative and the officers would just die, they would cringe because they seemed so fearful of the generals."

The media fears of the Army generals, journalists discovered, extended to a lot of little things. Scott Pelley, a CBS news correspondent, found his escorts in the 18th Airborne Corps had been instructed not to let the television crew shoot pictures of soldiers arguing. Steve Elfers, a photographer with the *Army Times*, was about to take a picture of a 1st Cavalry Division soldier with a rag wound around his head when his escort told him that the division commander, Maj. Gen. John H. Tilelli, had decreed that no pictures could be taken of troopers unless they had their helmets on and their chin straps buckled.

Escorts with me in the 3d Armored Division were given a little card with a Miranda-like warning that they were supposed to read to soldiers about to be interviewed. It instructed them that they didn't have to say anything if they didn't want to. The escorts, however, were too embarrassed to read it.

On Wednesday, February 27, as elements of VII Corps began to roll over the Republican Guard, it apparently occurred to the generals that, while they seemed to be in control of the little things, the big picture had gone blank. For the first time the Army provided helicopters to attempt to get copy and film from the reporters in the field. Despite six hours of searching, the choppers failed to find any of them. As Lieutenant Colonel Gleisberg explained, the problem was that the public affairs officers in his divisions didn't have any radios. By the time the helicopters reached the positions they had reported by field telephone, the units had moved on.

On Thursday, the day the war ended, some of the choppers were sent out again, managing to find only one unit. The Army diverted the rest of the helicopters to the task of picking up Iraqi prisoners, who were now coming in by the thousands. Meanwhile, a windstorm had knocked out a commercial fax facility that Colonel Mulvey had been preparing at King Khalid Military City—using funds donated by the Saudis. The fax was intended to eliminate the last leg of the courier system and thus to expedite filing stories, but there was no Army public affairs officer in the area with sufficient clout to get it running again.

"That finished us off," grumbles Colonel Mulvey. His assistant, Lt. Col. Larry F. Icenoggle, puts their experience this way: "I don't have any funny war stories. There was nothing that happened over there that was funny. You saw your worst fears coming true."

Journalists out on the battlefields also saw their worst fears coming true. They were in a no-win game that thwarted even the best preparations. Michael B. Hedges of the *Washington Times* had spent weeks in the field with the 1st Infantry Division trying to devise ways to avoid the pitfalls that he knew would appear once the ground war began.

He'd discovered, for example, that while his news reports before the war were taking three days to reach Dhahran, the Red Cross unit in his division had a fax that could send a message back in three minutes. He arranged for a courier to pick up his copy and take it back to that fax.

Colonel Mulvey hoped that experienced reporters would "bond" with unit commanders and get their assistance out in the field, and Mr. Hedges had done it. He had made an arrangement for access to the division's general during the war. He had a West Point educated captain driving an escort vehicle with a satellite-operated global positioning unit for navigation.

But once the war started, all of Mr. Hedges's careful preparations went awry. A CNN television crew, part of the last-minute influx of reporters, took Mr. Hedges's vehicle, leaving him and Robert P. Jordan, an Associated Press photographer, with a broken-down Ford Bronco with no navigation aids, no ignition system, and flashlights taped to each fender for lights. Armed guards suddenly appeared around the Red Cross fax machine, preventing its use. When Mr. Hedges drove his copy and Mr. Jordan's film back to a rear pickup point, they got lost and were unable to find their division for the crucial last two days of the war.

Following compass headings, their West Point captain managed to drive them straight into an Iraqi position. Other Iraqis had already given up, but these Iraqis were still fighting the war. Then the Bronco hit a machine gun tripod and blew a tire. There was a very, very tense moment as Mr. Hedges and his captain mounted the spare while Iraqi officers watched them through binoculars from 400 feet away.

"I knew we were in trouble from the beginning," says Mr. Jordan, who spent seven years as a National Guard public affairs officer before becoming a photographer. "You could see there wasn't any support from the top echelon. It could have worked but I don't think the Army wanted it to work."

Martha Teichner, a CBS correspondent and veteran of war coverage in such dangerous, strife-torn places as El Salvador, Northern Ireland, Beirut, and Romania, spent five weeks with her crew scouting out the possibilities for coverage in VII Corps. When Major Cook said they couldn't cover the 1st Armored Division because they lacked a vehicle, sleeping bags, lanterns, and heaters, Ms. Teichner's cameraman brought the equipment up from Dhahran.

Then they discovered that their courier, the Army driver assigned to bring their videotape back from the front, couldn't read maps. After repeatedly getting lost with him in the desert,

Ms. Teichner became convinced that there was little or no chance of her war stories getting back in time to be aired.

"I was worried that he would take the stuff and drive into a mine field. That would mean I would get him killed. I couldn't live with that," explains Ms. Teichner. So she and her crew left the field a few days before the ground war started as a "protest."

"I came back to Dhahran absolutely heartbroken, but there I was on television constantly. There was every incentive in this war to be a hotel warrior."

(Ms. Teichner's replacement, James Hattori, a CBS reporter based in Dallas, was picked up by Major Cook at an airport near VII Corps's rear base. Driving the new CBS crew back, he says, Major Cook became lost, and they spent the night at the airport. Mr. Hattori was unable to locate frontline units until after the war. When he did, he discovered there were no couriers. Most of his videotape did not arrive until four days after the war and was deemed obsolete. "Martha proved to be quite astute," he says.)

Two days before the war, John S. Mecklin, an investigative reporter from the *Houston Post*, arrived at the headquarters of the 3d Armored Division's second brigade escorted by one of the division's public affairs officers, a lieutenant. They were driving a diesel-powered Army van. The battered van, painted camouflage green to make it blend in with German forests, was identical to those carrying soldiers and reporters in the division's other two brigades. Although he had a letter from the division's commander assigning him to the brigade, Mr. Mecklin was told he was in an unauthorized vehicle and would have to leave.

When he objected, Mr. Mecklin said he was told by a staff sergeant that "if we tried to go forward that [the brigade's commander] Col. Robert W. Higgins would use his own .45 caliber sidearm to shoot the tires off our vehicle." Mr. Mecklin and his escort went back to division headquarters where he wrote several stories and phoned them back to VII Corps rear. When Mr. Mecklin arrived back in Dhahran on Saturday, two days after the war ended, he discovered that most of his stories were still stuck in VII Corps.

The scuttlebutt among the division's junior officers was that Colonel Higgins, a Vietnam veteran, still harbored bitter feelings that the press "lost" that war. A spokesman for the division said that Colonel Higgins had no comment about the Mecklin incident or on his general attitude toward the press.

If this war had an Ernie Pyle, it was probably Gregory Jaynes, a *Life* magazine reporter. He met a tank platoon of the 1st Cavalry Division—16 men—as they arrived at the docks in Dammam, Saudi Arabia, and offered to follow them through the course of the entire war and then follow them home.

Mr. Jaynes spent weeks in the field with the platoon and wrote about training amid "the heat, the flies, the snakes, and the almost lunar loneliness" of the desert. Then he went back to Texas to write moving stories about the impact of the Gulf crisis on their families and girlfriends.

When he arrived back in Saudi Arabia in December, Mr. Jaynes ran into an Army-built brick wall. He was told that the division's commander, Major General Tilelli, would not allow the reporter any further contacts with the platoon.

"It was devastating," says Mr. Jaynes, who thought he had the general's express approval for a whole series of articles about the platoon. "It was going to be a huge investment of time and money, whatever it took."

The general was adamant. He refused to give Mr. Jaynes an explanation and refused to meet with him about the matter. Other reporters who covered the division during the war say the scuttlebutt in the 1st Cav was that the general was upset by profanity in Jaynes's articles. Mr. Jaynes finds that hard to believe. "Soldiers use four letter words? Surprise, surprise. Some of their families had the articles laminated."

Maj. Jeff Phillips, spokesman for the 1st Cavalry, says the general's personal feelings about the articles weren't the reason that Mr. Jaynes couldn't return. The division was about to move north, he said, and the general decided that the arrangement with Mr. Jaynes "was a little more burdensome than the situation would permit." The need for secrecy, according to Major Phillips, was General Tilelli's main concern at the time.

Many reporters, myself included, were permitted to have some knowledge of the battle plans. By late January, for example, Douglas Jehl, a *Los Angeles Times* reporter, knew exactly where in Iraq the division he was covering, the 1st Armored Division, was going. He knew the attack plans in detail because he had been allowed to sit in on nightly brigade commanders' meetings.

This is not unusual in the history of American wars. Reporters landing in Normandy knew the rough outlines of the secret invasion plans and did not disclose them. What was unusual about Mr. Jehl's case, though, is that the secrets that he knew probably prevented the Army from carrying out a plan to transfer him, involuntarily, to another division.

In early February, Mr. Jehl wrote a story that said 50 jeeps had been stolen from the Army. A radio report based, incorrectly, on Mr. Jehl's pool report, said the 50 jeeps had all been stolen from the 1st Armored Division. Then Gen. H. Norman Schwarzkopf, the overall commander, called the division's commander, Maj. Gen. Ronald H. Griffith, wanting to know what the hell was going on. Then Mr. Jehl was told to pack up. He was being transferred out of VII Corps to the 101st Airborne.

"I objected on grounds of principle. As members of the pool, we'd been assigned to a particular division and the Army had no right to make an involuntary transfer," recalls Mr. Jehl. After carrying his protest up to the Army's top commander in Saudi Arabia, Lt. Gen. John J. Yeosock, Mr. Jehl was told he could stay.

General Griffith said that he did order Mr. Jehl removed from his division but changed his mind before hearing from General Yeosock. "I later grew to value his skills as a reporter," he said. Mr. Jehl thinks the Army's original scheme may have been to send him back to Dhahran, but it was thwarted by the generals' awareness that he had already been told the battle plans. "It never occured to them that I would say no [to the transfer]."

The story Mr. Jehl filed on Thursday, February 28, about the end of the ground war reached the *Los Angeles Times* on Sunday. By ordinary news standards that kind of delay is unacceptable, but by Army standards in this war it was pretty good. John Gaps, an Associated Press photographer working with the 7th Combat Engineers Brigade, sent one packet of film out with a courier on the first day of the war and for some unknown reason got it back on the third day. Another batch of film, shot at the outset of the war, arrived in Dhahran on March 30, more than a month later. "I have these beautiful pictures," he says, "and nobody will ever see them."

For journalists, the enormous delays were the hidden enemy out in the field. They annihilated the news. Not many of us focused on the problem out in the combat units, however. There were other things to worry about.

Bill Gannon, a reporter for the Newark *Star-Ledger*, says his Army escort simply dropped him off at the tent of the commander of the "Tiger Brigade," a unit drawn from the 2d Armored Division in Texas to operate in a joint task force with the

Marines. He had a choice: He could be on the cutting edge of the battle or go back to the rear with the escort (who told him he needed to go back to assure that the couriers would get the copy back). The commander, Col. John Silvester, told Mr. Gannon: "If you go with me, you will see everything we see, but there will be no safe place."

Mr. Gannon, 33, was scared. He was up all night worrying about it, but finally concluded he had to go with the colonel. "I realized how precious a position I was in. I felt I kind of owed it to history, owed it to my newspaper, owed it to the people [other reporters] back in Dhahran who were tearing their hair out trying to get into the field. Once I got past that point, I was okay."

The reporter saw rolling tank battles and wrote firsthand accounts of the Tiger Brigade's dramatic dash across the desert to cut off the so-called highway of death to Basra. Some of his best copy didn't make it back to Newark until March 3, much too late to be used. And some of it, he says, never arrived at all.

He is still proud of his experiences with the brigade but feels that Army public affairs people let him down. "The Tiger Brigade people were angry when I told them most of the news was about the Marines. They asked 'Did you write about all the tank battles we were in?'"

The few accounts of the Army's tank battles that did make it back to the States in time to be used got there without going through public affairs channels at all. James Wooten, an ABC reporter, remembers crawling into his sleeping bag with a satisfied feeling late Wednesday night.

Mr. Wooten had great experiences. He had shots of the battles and footage of an entire Iraqi company that had opted to surrender to his television crew. Suddenly Mr. Wooten had a galvanizing thought. The brigade commander, a big amiable man named Col. Leroy Goff, had mentioned that he had no military mission the next day. "Jesus, it's over," thought Mr. Wooten. "I've got to get out of here."

He put on his boots and went back to the colonel, who was still up after 72 hours of moving and fighting. Mr. Wooten told him "the stuff I've got here is going to end up in the archives unless I get out of here and get it on the air tomorrow." The colonel responded, "I'll see what I can do."

At dawn one of the division's Blackhawk helicopters arrived and flew Mr. Wooten and his precious cargo back to Dhahran, where he arrived in time to go on live on "Good Morning America."

The following day a similar deal was struck in the division's adjoining 1st brigade, where an Associated Press reporter, Fred Bayles, and I made the argument that if we didn't get a helicopter out, the news value of the brigade's running 42-hour battle against the Republican Guards' Tawalkana Division would be lost forever. That would be unfair to the brigade, we asserted, for it had made history.

It was a tense moment for me. It was late Thursday evening and we were God knows where in the northern Kuwaiti desert. The war was over, and the deadline for the *Wall Street Journal*'s Friday edition was approaching. (There is no Saturday or Sunday *Wall Street Journal*.) Col. Bill Nash's entire staff, a group of majors, captains, and our own public affairs escort, was arrayed against us. They ticked off their reasons. It was dark. There was no approved flight plan. It would be hard to find fuel for the helicopter. The general hadn't given permission, and on and on.

As his field radios screamed and crackled in the background, the colonel sat in a corner of his field tent, one leg draped over a chair, pensively chewing on a cigar stub. He remained noncommittal until one of his underlings announced, perhaps with too much of an air of finality, that there would be no helicopter available that night. "I'm going to make it fucking happen!" rasped Colonel Nash. Within two hours we were landing in Saudi Arabia next to an MCI tent with a satellite telephone hookup, a place for soldiers to call home, a place for reporters to redeem themselves.

In retrospect, these are fairy tales. The more typical war stories of journalists who covered the Army resemble John Balzar's of the *Los Angeles Times*. Mr. Balzar, an ABC crew, and reporters from Reuters and *Time* magazine were landed by helicopter at the wrong site and spent the last night of the war "with a unit who didn't even know who we were."

They were six miles away from the Apache helicopter unit they were supposed to interview when their escort, Lt. Col. Bob Perrich, flew off in the helicopter that had brought them. Ironically, Lieutenant Colonel Perrich was also the man responsible for setting up the forward-based commercial fax machine that might have shortcut the pony express and preserved more of the Army's side of the story, had it kept operating.

But the wind had blown down the tent Tuesday night, while the lieutenant colonel was off flying somewhere; although a high-ranking public affairs officer, who didn't have specific escort duties, he even flew on a mission to take Iraqi prisoners back from the front. "I wanted to look my enemy in the face after 20 years in the Army," he explained to the reporters he had left behind.

Lieutenant Colonel Perrich's airborne adventures did not sit well with those who ran the Joint Information Bureau back in Dhahran. "Had Perrich stayed there he could have stood on somebody's chest until they got the phones and the fax back in operation," complains Lieutenant Colonel Icenoggle. "Every problem we had was magnified because this was such a short-term war."

Asked about that, Lieutenant Colonel Perrich asserts he was flying around planning for the long term, scouting future sites for desert airfields that might have been needed had the war lasted longer. "I did my job as I understood it."

Perhaps the best summation of the experience of dealing with the Army's version of public affairs comes from Ms. Teichner, the CBS reporter who reluctantly left the battlefield before the shooting began:

"You've got incompetence from the bottom up and you've got resistance from the top down and it met where we were, in the pool. It all came together, and it was disastrous."

Chapter 3

The Marines: Business Is News

Reporters question Marine Lt. Gen. Walter E. Boomer during the ground war. From left: Denis Gray (AP); Colin Nickerson (Boston Globe); Jeff Franks (Reuters); General Boomer; Susan Sachs (Newsday); and Molly Moore (Washington Post). (U.S. Marine Corps photo by Col. John M. Shotwell)

On the first evening of the ground war, Marine L. Cpl. Brett W. Beard was handed a pouch containing a CNN television crew's videotape and a *Los Angeles Times* photographer's film rolls depicting the dramatic first moments of the war.

It had been an amazing day: Marine assault units expecting as much as 50 percent casualties breaching the feared Saddam Wall went charging into Kuwait almost unchallenged. They found that the main hazard was Iraqi soldiers trying to kiss them as they were giving up.

The Marines had developed a much better plan than the Army for getting news back from the front, but plans only go so far in what the famous Prussian military theorist, Carl von Clausewitz, called "the fog of war"—the inherent chaos of swiftly moving events. As the light began to fade that evening, the "fog" descended on the plan for Corporal Beard's mission.

He was supposed to hitch a ride on an ammunition truck going back to the large Marine logistic base on the Saudi side of the border, but as he walked around in the gathering darkness, he began to realize there were no trucks going back.

The breaching of enemy lines had been so uneventful that no ammunition resupply was needed. There were 15 miles of barren desert between Corporal Beard and his destination. He had no compass and no food. But he knew what had to be done, so he began figuring out a way to do it.

Finding south was easy. The fiercely blazing Kuwaiti oil fields to the north looked like a permanently setting sun. Keeping the fires behind him, he just kept walking through the night and through the next day. At one point, almost overcome with dizziness, he abandoned his pack with his personal belongings, but not his rifle or the pouch.

The rifle was kept to deal with bypassed units of Iraqi soldiers that he knew were still roaming the desert. As for the pouch: "I just knew that every moment when I couldn't get that back, people in the States wouldn't know what was going on," recalls Corporal Beard, who has since been decorated with a Navy Achievement Medal for his effort.

While platoons of Army colonels, majors, and captains were absorbed in a losing battle with the Army's collapsing system for getting news back, a comparative handful of Marine public affairs officers were making their system work with fewer people and fewer resources, often relying on the ingenuity of enlisted men and women. Although the Army's best effort was getting the news back from VII Corps within 72 hours, a Marine chief warrant officer, Eric R. Carlson, had devised a way of getting the news back from the 1st Marine Division in minutes.

How did he do it? Pete Williams, the assistant secretary of defense for public affairs, took a team of Pentagon officials to examine CWO Carlson's secret. The 37-year-old Marine showed them a battered Zenith laptop computer on which reporters wrote their stories. CWO Carlson would then take the computer disk over to the Marine field communications center and send it by E-mail to the Marine headquarters at Jubail. There it was printed and sent via fax to the Joint Information Bureau in Dhahran. Zap, and the news was on its way home.

The differences between the two services' skills in handling public affairs were so vast that reporters sometimes wondered whether they represented different countries. One major result of these differences was that the Marines garnered most of the publicity, skewing the coverage of the ground war, in which they performed a much smaller, supporting role to the Army.

The Marines never seemed to get enough media people in the field; they were still badgering the Joint Information Bureau in Dhahran for more journalists, even as the ground war kicked off. Army commanders only grudgingly accepted journalists assigned to them and, at times, could not conceal their deep-seated hostility toward the press.

The peculiarly divergent philosophies begin at the very top. The entire Marine expeditionary force was commanded by Lieutenant General Boomer, the smooth-talking former head of the Marine public affairs office. That could never happen in the Army, where the public affairs chore is regarded as a dead-end job, a career path that does not lead to a major command of troops.

The Marines think so much of the public affairs job that, in a crisis, they give it to whoever can get it done. That is why, at the end of the war, sublieutenants such as CWO Carlson were commandeering helicopters from colonels. That could never, ever happen in the Army, which has been painstakingly structured so that public affairs officers, regardless of their position in the hierarchy, must always beg for resources from people who outrank them.

It is not that Marines love the press. "We didn't view the news media as a group of people we were supposed to schmooze," is the way CWO Carlson puts it. "We regarded them as an environmental feature of the battlefield, kind of like the rain. If it rains you operate wet."

Col. John M. Shotwell, General Boomer's public affairs officer, notes that journalists in the field require extra logistical support, sometimes got in the way during training, and always presented a potential security threat. Edgy field commanders, having to train bored troops in the desert heat on morale-killing subjects such as preparations for chemical warfare, were not exactly clamoring for news coverage. "The last thing they wanted to deal with at this time was a gaggle of journalists."

But a gaggle was what they got because the Marines decided early on that journalists were inevitable and that, when properly handled, they helped develop strong public support for the Marines' mission. "As the months wore on, a phenomenon developed [that] none of us public affairs officers really expected. Some of our commanders actually began to enjoy having reporters around," concludes Colonel Shotwell, who later summed up his experiences in an article in the *Marine Corps Gazette* entitled, "The Fourth Estate as a Force Multiplier."[1]

It was Colonel Shotwell who cleared the public affairs decks for action, transferring a captain out of the 1st Marine Division's public affairs post and giving the position to CWO Carlson, who, among his other talents, has a genius for scrounging. For the Marines, that was crucial.

If you are the public affairs officer for an Army division, you get tents, cots, heaters, vehicles, cadres of enlisted men, and lots of supplies. When CWO Carlson looked in the Marine Corps's table of organization, he found that division public affairs officers are entitled to a desk. That was it. A desk. His had been shipped in from Hawaii, and it was the wrong kind.

CWO Carlson started expanding with some borrowed jeeps. He then acquired a truck, which he traded for a tent, which he furnished with the laptop, which came from undisclosed sources. "It's safe to say that our means of getting equipment to do the job was kind of ad hoc, and in some cases a little shady, to be frank."

After that he started scrounging for reporters. The original agreement passed down from the Pentagon was that the Marines and the Army would each get a pool of 18 journalists. By the time the war started, the Marines had worked their share up to 53, but Marine commanders knew that 22 of them were floating offshore to cover an event that would never be: the amphibious landing that was a feint to fool the Iraqis.

That lent more urgency to efforts to recruit reporters for the Marine ground missions that remained. Maj. Jay C. Farrar was hustling reporters for the 2d Marine Division and, on the eve of the war, General Boomer himself sent out a letter inviting six reporters to accompany his mobile command post.

Five of us who were invited by General Boomer were either already out in the field with Army units or out of the country, but, curiously, reporter Molly Moore of the *Washington Post* was waiting for the phone to ring in her Dhahran International Hotel room. Although under the pool system the *Post* already had its assigned quota of reporters in the field, Ms. Moore rode with General Boomer's mobile command post throughout the war.

At one point, when her computer's batteries failed, she typed her story on a Marine computer. When that failed, she dictated a story over a field telephone to Jubail where a Marine retyped it and faxed it to Dhahran. "We basically did whatever it took to get [the] product back as fast as [we] possibly could," explains Major Farrar.

By late Tuesday night, the Marines had captured Kuwait City Airport, surrounded the city, and discovered that the Iraqi resistance had collapsed. This was a great story, but Kirk Spitzer, the Gannett News Service reporter who was covering it, was trapped in a foxhole in a howling desert windstorm as his deadline approached. No problem. The Marines set up a portable satellite phone, and Mr. Spitzer dictated his report directly to his office in Washington, which faxed a copy back to the press center in Dhahran.

There was no radio reporter around to cover the capture of Kuwait City Airport either, but the Marines had a ready solution for that. "We got a call from a Marine [chief warrant] officer using a field phone. He was reading from a wire service report of the capture," recalls John T. Lyons, the manager of the radio pool in Dhahran. "We did a question and answer with him. It was very timely."

Unlike the Army, the Marines understood that timeliness is the essence of news. "We had the first footage out of U.S. troops in the ground war," boasts Linda Pattillo, an ABC correspondent who lived with the Marines in the field for six weeks. "Our PAO [public affairs officer] was so anxious to get our footage out he ran out and flagged down a medevac chopper."

.Although Kuwait City was off-limits to U.S. troops, it wasn't to General Boomer. He took Ms. Moore and an entourage of other reporters, including Jeff Franks, a reporter for Reuters, into the newly liberated city with him on Wednesday, ostensibly to check out the Marines who had been trapped in the U.S. embassy. "If any experience made the long five months of preparation worthwhile, that was it," exults Mr. Franks.

On Wednesday night, Army units finished their historic, long-distance flanking movement and fought the biggest tank battles of the war. This generated little news because the Army was operating in what amounted to a self-imposed news blackout. Meanwhile, the Marines captured the airwaves, holding forth before hundreds of journalists from all over the world at Kuwait City Airport. "I decided the pool system was defunct, so I began accepting unilaterals," explains CWO Carlson. "Unilaterals" were journalists operating outside the pool system. Some had abandoned their Army units to get to Kuwait City.

CWO Carlson produced the show at the airport despite the fact that he had been up 96 hours straight. But his adrenaline was pumping; he had acquired massive new powers to scrounge. In the Marines' new mobile warfare doctrine, resources are supposed to shift quickly to the *shwerpunkt*, another Clausewitzian term meaning the point of main effort. Since the fighting was over, Maj. Gen. James M. Myatt, commander of the 1st Marine Division, deemed his public affairs officer to be the division's *shwerpunkt*.

"I walked up to the division operations officer, a guy who would barely give me the time of day and said I wanted a map redone. I wanted them to set up a command post for a news conference," recalls CWO Carlson. "I went to the air officer and said I wanted a helicopter because I wanted a television news crew up in it. That's the kind thing that happens when the PAO becomes the *shwerpunkt*."

So General Myatt went up in the helicopter with the television crew attached to CBS's anchor, Dan Rather, and showed them some of the sites of the Marines' tank battles. He made a big splash on the "CBS Evening News." CWO Carlson's crews set up generators and portable lights amid the looted ruins of the airport's main terminal building for the press conference, which proved to be one of the major media events of the war. CWO Carlson even had Italian journalist and celebrity Oriana Fallaci following him around that evening, bumming cigars.

The Marines' system was by no means perfect. "The Marines on the ground that I dealt with were tremendous. They made extraordinary efforts to get tapes back to the distribution center," recalls Peter Van Sant, a correspondent for CBS. Nonetheless, he says, one of his tapes was delayed two days, two were delayed six days, and two never came back at all. (The Marines say they carefully logged the tapes in and have no explanation for the loss.)

"It was the most devastating moment of my career to get back to Dhahran," explains Mr. Van Sant. "We'd risked our butts. Our colleagues just kinda looked at us and said, 'Where were you during the war?'"

Reporters who worked with the Marines—with the exception of Ms. Moore of the *Washington Post*—discovered they had to live like the Marine troops. This was another of the major differences in covering the two services.

For the most part, journalists covering the Army slept in public affairs tents on cots and could stay up all night writing stories. During the war we carried our gear in vehicles and often slept in them. Journalists covering the Marines almost invariably had to dig and sleep in foxholes, enduring the desert rains without tents. They carried their gear on their backs. At 5 P.M., when the desert light began to fade, so did writing because the Marines wouldn't take the risk of having reporters' flashlights reveal their position.

"The Marines wanted us to suffer along with them. They told us that was a way to build respect," says Mr. Franks of Reuters. "It sort of worked. I always thought there was sort of an element of almost viciousness about it. They were suffering, but they wanted us to, too."

"It's not a bad idea as a journalist to go out and spend six weeks in the desert to live the way the grunts do and see how they live. It was confining, but a lot of us were able to do good stories," says ABC's Ms. Pattillo, the daughter of a former Marine, who quickly became adept at the art of scrounging. She gave cartons of cigarettes to grunts who were more than happy to dig her foxhole. For the price of a few ABC-TV baseball caps, she got a cot to put in it.

While some of her stories were negative, that didn't seem to bother the Marines, she said. "Just because some Marine is on TV complaining about the chow doesn't mean he's complaining about the war. They didn't feel as much as the Army did that one bad portrayal of a soldier was going to hurt the whole corps."

Lieutenant General Boomer says, "I don't know why it turned out the way it did on the Army's side. As far as we were concerned, what we did seemed to be fairly natural and the right thing to do. It's undergirded to a degree by the belief that the American people have a right to know, and we the Marines are trying to do the best we can to let people take a look at us."

Note

[1]Col. John M. Shotwell, "The Fourth Estate as a Force Multiplier," *Marine Corps Gazette* (July 1991): 71–79.

Chapter 4

The Pools: Business Is Frustrating

Reporters check the media pool schedules on the bulletin board in the Joint Information Bureau (JIB) at the Dhahran International Hotel. (U.S. Army photo by the 49th PAD)

Early in February, Joseph L. Galloway, a senior writer for *U.S. News and World Report*, was granted an interview in Riyadh with the supreme commander of the Gulf War, Gen. H. Norman Schwarzkopf.

General Schwarzkopf gave many interviews during the war. He often used the opportunity as another lever of control over the media, which he watched with an ever-vigilant eye. Reporters whose stories he liked got interviews. Those whose stories didn't pass muster with the general often found the opportunity postponed, sometimes indefinitely.

The general especially liked the stories of Mr. Galloway, a 49-year-old former United Press International wire service reporter whom the general had known since the Vietnam War. Mr. Galloway was one of the few reporters sent to Saudi Arabia with prior combat experience. He had also been to Dhahran and had seen the shortcomings of the system being used to get journalists into the pools that were being sent north to cover the ground war.

At the U.S. military's Joint Information Bureau (JIB) in the Dhahran International Hotel, news organizations coordinated the matter of who went out into the field. If a Marine division had "slots" or availabilities for, say, three reporters, a television crew, a radio reporter, and three photographers, coordinators selected by the organizations of photographers, radio, print, and television correspondents would come up with the names. After that, the JIB's military coordinators, representing all four services, would issue equipment and transport them out to the division.

A pecking order had been established by the time Mr. Galloway arrived, and he found that his magazine already had filled its assigned quota of "slots" with combat units in the field.

As Mr. Galloway discovered, the quota was necessary because there were hundreds of journalists waiting in Dhahran to go out to the battlefield and not enough combat units willing to take them. A Byzantine system of pool rules had evolved, and it soon became one of the factors inhibiting the news flow out of the Gulf.

While the rules weren't all greeted with enthusiasm by journalists, there was one rule that nearly all of us felt was inviolate: that news organizations should pick the journalists going out into the battlefield, not the generals. General Schwarzkopf made short shrift of that rule. As Mr. Galloway recalls: "He [Schwarzkopf] says, 'I know what you want, and I'm going to give it to you.'"

General Schwarzkopf then ordered that a slot be quietly created for Mr. Galloway at the side of the general leading General Schwarzkopf's old unit, the Army's 24th Mechanized Infantry Division. It was a complete evasion of the pool system, which General Schwarzkopf's own office had helped design. The system had taken months of negotiations between the Pentagon and Washington bureau chiefs attempting to ensure fair access to the battlefield. It had been subverted with an imperial handshake.

While other reporters covering the Army had great difficulty getting their copy back, Mr. Galloway's prose shot back at the speed of light. "An officer who shall go nameless faxed all my copy and sent it to a satellite point where it went to my office," he recalls.

Another reporter with the 24th, Ronald L. Martz of Cox Newspapers, had also gotten there by circumventing the pool system. He had a secret deal with the 24th's commander, Gen.

Barry McCaffrey. Mr. Martz's pool reports, though, made it appear that he was watching a different war from Mr. Galloway.

On February 25, Mr. Martz reported that the 24th hit a mostly undefended sector of the Iraqi lines, well to the west of the main Iraqi forces. It encountered "few Iraqi tanks, troops, or bunkers" and no obstacles, such as mines or even concertina wire.

Yet Mr. Galloway found the 24th's performance "miraculous." He called it the war's "toughest mission" and "the greatest cavalry charge in history."

Shortly before strapping on his rucksack, Mr. Galloway also found time to write a glowing portrait of General Schwarzkopf—"a general who knows soldiers and loves them, who knows war and hates it."

Mr. Galloway denies the general's patronage had any effect on his writing. It was, he admits, a fundamental violation of the pool system. "I can see your point," he says, "but a guy hands me this, and I'm not going to say no."

This was a war where a number of people in the press couldn't help helping themselves despite conditions that forced us to agree to a pool. In essence, a pool means that all of the news products from the war be shared, but "beggar thy neighbor" was often closer to the reality under which we operated. For a time before the ground war and shortly afterward, I was coordinator for the largest pool in Dhahran, the print pool, one of a half dozen or so journalists who made the mistake of volunteering for that thankless task. Our internal fighting never stopped.

The second major pool, the photographers' pool, operated more peacefully under the iron grip of its cabal of five leaders, but they had one running shootout that kept everyone on edge. The third pool, the television pool, arrived equipped with its own czar. To most of us, it seemed quiet, too, but a behind-the-scenes battle among the networks erupted early in the war that would ultimately constrict the news flow to the outside world.

Reporters in the smallest pool, the radio pool, were busy "holding out information on each other and vying for pool slots," according to John T. Lyons, general manager of news operations for ABC radio. This went on until the radio networks copied the structure of the television pool and sent in Mr. Lyons as czar. After that, Mr. Lyons says, "I basically gave the orders and reported to all the networks."

All four pools had offices on the upper two floors of the Dhahran International Hotel, near the U.S. military's JIB and a similar informational bureau set up by the Saudis. In the luxurious lobby and over the well-set tables of the hotel's dining rooms, the internal politics of the media were often the primary topic of discussion. Despite the fact that the hotel sat in the midst of the biggest air base in Saudi Arabia and was the arrival point for many of the troops, there were many times when the war seemed secondary.

Journalists arriving in Dhahran started out by registering themselves with one of the media pools. Once they worked up to the top of the lists maintained by pool coordinators, they were eligible to go out in the field to serve in the combat pools, set up and managed by U.S. forces. Each of the media pools soon developed its own political character and established rules for determining priorities.

The television pool was an autocracy. Tom Giusto, an ABC assignment editor in Washington, was sent by the four networks to Dhahran to be the pool coordinator and final arbiter of any disputes. For the duration of the war, Mr. Giusto's paycheck came jointly from ABC, CBS, NBC, and CNN, a move intended to immunize him from any charges of special dealing on behalf of his own network.

The folklore is that television people are more used to pooled coverage than other journalists. "We are accustomed to camera coverage pools," points out George Watson, Washington bureau chief for ABC. "We are not accustomed to reporting pools and indeed we resisted strenuously."

The three traditional networks—ABC, CBS, and NBC—resisted even more strenuously after the air war started when they saw their correspondents doing battlefield stand ups on CNN. "Competitively that's not acceptable to us," explains Mr. Watson. "We clarified the rules to make it clear that pooling did not mean you had access to voice and person that another network had as their exclusive correspondent."

This was one of two problems that the pool's czar, Mr. Giusto, couldn't resolve. After several stormy sessions, network moguls voted 3–1 to make a change. After that the pool got the videotape shot in the field, but not the network's stars to narrate it.

"We were happy to put the CBS correspondent on the air with a pool report. We were getting all sorts of mileage out of this," explains Bill Headline, CNN's Washington bureau chief.

"We had those goddamn reports on as soon as they were in. The other networks, not having the airtime, changed the rule. Philosophically, it deprived the public of more firsthand reports from the Gulf."

After that, a lot of the CBS, NBC, and ABC reportage that had only been seen on CNN wound up on the cutting-room floor. There was more news coming in from the field than the three networks could handle. That was Mr. Giusto's second big headache: the Army's plane from King Khalid Military City and Marine couriers from Jubail delivered about eight hours of videotape from crews operating with combat units every night, starting at around 10 P.M.

Because the television pool in Dhahran had only one satellite link, it could transmit only half of the videotape, roughly four hours worth, to New York before the deadlines for evening news shows at 2:30 A.M.

"It all got sent eventually, but we fed the newest, most dramatic material first," explains Mr. Giusto. "I would take a quick look at the date of the videotape, look at the script, and then make the decision of which one to feed first."

Since the most delayed videotapes usually came from the Army, the majority of its coverage was never shown. Mr. Giusto says he tried to contain the nightly logjam by urging field crews "to minimize their shooting as much as possible." But some crews never seemed to get the word.

The jam-ups and arguments within the television pool were minuscule compared to what was going on in the photo pool, a plutocracy run by photo editors from the three news magazines—*Time, Newsweek*, and *U.S. News and World Report*—and two major wire services, the Associated Press and Reuters.

"There were nights when we had as many as 180 rolls of film coming in. That means over 6,000 images," explains Donald Mell, an Associated Press photo editor who coordinated the pool during the ground war. Editors from the five ruling organizations would sit down and winnow them down to about 20 pictures, he said, which would become the official photo pool report for that day.

Then both wire services would transmit the same 20 pictures to some 1,500 newspaper customers throughout the U.S. "That's essentially what the [wire photo transmission] system can hold," explains Mr. Mell.

"There was a lot of respect among the professionals in that room for each other," adds Mr. Mell. "There wasn't a lot of disagreement. Nobody worked there on their own agenda. I said the agenda here is what's good for one of us is good for all of us."

The tranquility in the photo pool was hopelessly shattered on January 18, however, when a special, Pentagon-dispatched Air Force C-141 carrying 126 more journalists arrived in Dhahran to cover the war. The crowd included dozens of photographers from individual newspapers, each eager to get his or her own "shooter" out in the field despite the fact that all the available photo slots were already filled.

Then the Knight-Ridder/*Chicago Tribune* Newswire, which serves 50 papers in the U.S., took up the cudgels for the newspaper photographers and demanded to be cut in on the leadership of the pool.

"Granted we were Johnny-come-lately, but we showed up in considerable force. I shouted and screamed and stomped up and down until I was blue in the face," recalls Charles Borst, director of the Knight-Ridder photo service. But the pool leaders, operating under a system that required a 5–0 vote to make a change, rejected him, and Mr. Borst was barred from the editing room.

The pool's rules provided that Knight-Ridder could look at film sent in by newspaper photographers, but not at film shot by anybody else. Meanwhile, what Mr. Borst calls the big five were able to pick from among all the news photographers' pictures.

The news wire's size and stable of photographers made it bigger than Reuters in the U.S. or some of the newsmagazines in Dhahran, yet it wound up with no say in the daily pick of 20 pictures selected from the daily incoming flood of film rolls.

"We were asking, 'How do you know that the frame you selected is the one that we want?'" recalls Mr. Borst. He became so angry one night that he kicked a hole in a box of styrofoam packing material. Hearing the noise, the Dhahran International Hotel's bomb squad appeared, checking the rooms along his hallway. There was always tension of one sort or another in the hotel, beginning with the fear that it was a perfect target for terrorists.

Dhahran was then also under nightly attack from Iraqi Scud missiles, and the photographers' arguments were often interrupted by air raids, sending participants running down to the hotel's basement. There they were unable to resume the debate because they were wearing their gas masks.

"There were some arguments. A lot of long hours and sleep deprivation. A lot of these arguments should have never happened," believes Pat Benic, photo editor for Reuters, who still resents the sudden influx of newspaper photographers. "A lot of them came off the plane and thought they were going to get a photo pass for the 50-yard line."

While the political character of the television and photo pools was set early in the buildup to the war, the print pool oscillated from pure democracy to plutocracy to a dictatorship, depending upon who was running it.

The print pool was founded by the earliest journalist settlers in Dhahran, members of the nation's ten largest news organizations. They had arrived in August and September, just as the Gulf crisis got under way. Its members were reporters from three wire services—Associated Press, Reuters, and United Press International—three newsmagazines—*Time, Newsweek,* and *U.S. News and World Report*—and four major papers—*New York Times, Wall Street Journal, Washington Post,* and *Los Angeles Times.*

To the smaller news organizations that later began to flock to Dhahran, the founders often appeared to be an insurmountable obstacle to getting out in the field. In the endless round of arguments that followed, they starred as the "Sacred Ten," which broadened into the "Sacred Sixteen" as other major news organizations, including the *Boston Globe, Chicago Tribune,* Knight-Ridder, *USA Today,* the Gannett News Service, and Cox Newspapers began to work their way into the clique that dominated the pool.

"Nobody seemed to express their needs to me in a low voice," recalls Nicholas Horrock, the Washington bureau chief for the *Chicago Tribune,* who was pool coordinator during most of the air and ground war. Like the rest of us who coordinated the pool at various times, Mr. Horrock had people lobbying him almost 24 hours a day.

The competitive pressure was intense. There were 39 print reporters in the field, and at least twice that number wanted to go out. Editors of little papers were fuming. They had spent enormous amounts of money to get reporters to Dhahran, only to have them wait in hotel rooms.

Editors of larger papers, such as the *New York Times,* were screaming because they had sent a platoon of reporters, but under the pool's rules most could only get one into a combat slot at a time.

The *New York Times* bureau chief in Dhahran, R. W. Apple, who seemed to spend most of his time in his hotel room studying pool reports and watching televised briefings, used one of his rare appearances in the JIB to threaten its director, Col. William Mulvey. Either Colonel Mulvey got the *Times* a better combat pool slot, Mr. Apple told Colonel Mulvey in front of a crowd of junior officers, or Mr. Apple would arrange to have Dick Cheney, the secretary of defense, fire Colonel Mulvey from his job. (The threat had no effect. Mr. Apple insisted later he was misunderstood.)

Then there were the 300 foreign journalists milling in and out of Dhahran. They were constantly badgering everybody for a chance to get out into the field, but the U.S. military would make no provisions for them until all U.S. journalists were satisfied. (The exceptions were two British journalists allowed to cover U.S. Army and Marine units.)

Hungry for any scrap of news, the foreign reporters sometimes made off with the original copies of field reports, forcing the print pool to set up an office with a staff, a set of guarded mailboxes, a fax, and two copy machines to assure that U.S. pool organizations got the copy their reporters had written.

Although pool reports from journalists in the field were meant to provide pieces of the big picture on the battlefield, some reporters simply didn't bother filling in the rest. "Some hacks became shameless pool hounds, rewriting other people's stories and filing them as their own with a Saudi dateline and no acknowledgment of source," recalls James Meek of the British newspaper, the *Scotsman*. He calls it "fairly desperate behavior," which aptly describes some of the American practitioners of the art. In two cases they put their bylines on stories from *Wall Street Journal* reporters without changing so much as a word.

In the midst of all this, Mr. Horrock made the dismal discovery that the reporters who were out in the field didn't work very well as a pool. This became clear on January 30, when an Iraqi tank column invaded Khafji, a small Saudi border town. In historical terms, the battle means little, but at the time it was the hottest news story going. Mr. Horrock could make little sense out of it from reading the pool reports.

"The pool reports that did come in were absolute mumbo jumbo," recalls Mr. Horrock. "Some had no sense of time in them, some were impressionistic. Some people were out there developing features, which would have been fine, but 20 other people back in Dhahran were depending on them."

Mr. Horrock wanted more professional reporters out in the field. "I kept arguing that we were having the wrong people in the wrong places, but whenever I said that, nine little papers jumped down my neck."

The problem was exemplified by Jane DeLynn, a reporter for *Mirabella* (a women's magazine). She was among the reporters on the list waiting to get out in the field. Under the print pool's rules, the list had to be exhausted before the big papers could get a second reporter into a combat unit. Once Ms. DeLynn got her slot, she spent most of her time writing about the sex lives of female soldiers and the drugs used by medical units.

"She shouldn't have been out there," asserts Arthur Spiegleman, assistant bureau chief in Dhahran for Reuters, who spent 20 hours a day sifting through the pool reports for serious news. "People like that aren't serving their function. The pool is a camera's eye. You're coming up with information for everybody. People out there are in a privileged position to see something, but a lot of the stuff that came through was unusable. It was throwawayable."

The only solution print pool coordinators could find for what came to be known as "the *Mirabella* problem," was to create more combat slots. This was tough in January and early February when the military refused to allow any additions.

The spirit of democracy in the print pool peaked in January when one of Mr. Horrock's predecessors in the pool coordinator's job, Joseph Albright of Cox Newspapers, spent days wrestling with the *Mirabella* problem. Some news organizations, such as the Scripps Howard and Copley newspaper chains, had acquired two slots by having different member newspapers sign up. Mr. Albright took those slots away and gave them to smaller news organizations waiting to get people out in the field.

Mr. Albright soon discovered, however, that some problems were beyond his capacity to solve. For example, the second Copley reporter, Susan Walker, insisted on staying out in the field. Because she had won the favor of Maj. Gen. Paul E. Funk, commander of the 3d Armored Division—about whom she'd written several flattering reports—the JIB's military coordinators couldn't pry her out. She even refused a summons from her editor to leave.

Then there was the daily airing of David A. Fulgham's predicament. He was a reporter for the magazine *Aviation Week* but was unable to get out in the field to cover the air war because *Time*, *Newsweek*, and *U.S. News and World Report* had a rule that said that they were the only magazines entitled to combat slots.

"I'm not a combative person," explains Mr. Fulgham, who spent all day lobbying for his cause. "But this was so horrible you just had to be horrible to get anywhere with anyone."

Unlike the other pools, which had managers paid to run them, the print pool was run by volunteers. Mr. Albright, like the rest of us, had to file stories despite the fact that running the pool was more than a full-time job. In the back of his mind, as he continued to grapple with the problem of slots, Mr. Albright had the nagging feeling that we were all overlooking something, something fundamental.

It was the communications problem. "Some of us saw this coming, but we didn't pursue it," he admits. "If we'd only been more aggressive, if we had insisted that every pool had to have a guaranteed line of communications in from the field, I think a lot of our later problems would have been solved."

But they weren't. After Mr. Horrock took over, he and the other pool coordinators kept pounding away on the slots problem until one Saturday in February when they confronted the Pentagon's assistant secretary for public affairs, Pete Williams, during a visit to Dhahran. The pool chiefs convinced him that he ought to double the slots for journalists in the battlefield.

"The biggest point we made was that they [the Pentagon] were killing their own history," recalls Mr. Horrock. Another concern troubling Mr. Williams was that if he didn't expand the numbers of reporters working in pools, a lot of news organizations would send them up to the battlefield anyway, endangering their lives and perhaps fouling up battle plans.

As the additional reporters—most of them being absorbed by a last-minute decision to expand Army slots—lined up for their equipment, Mr. Horrock sat down with JIB coordinators to work out the next problem.

They had to determine the makeup of the pool that would cover the Marines' amphibious landing. It was an action that was never carried out, but at the time it was the most sought-after combat pool. The simplest way to form it was to take two existing groups of journalists that had been covering the Navy and merge them to form the pool that would supposedly hit the beach with the Marines.

When George P. Rodrigue, a Pulitzer Prize–winning reporter for the *Dallas Morning News,* learned that everyone else from the two earlier pools had been folded into the new Marine landing pool, he thought something was fishy. He called Mr. Horrock.

"Nick told me something that I will personally remember for some time," recalls Mr. Rodrigue. "He said he had decided that it would be in the best interest of history, journalism, and the American people if someone from a larger newspaper covered that particular pool."

Mr. Rodrigue says he didn't learn until later that Mr. Horrock had given the slot to David Evans, a reporter from the *Chicago Tribune,* Mr. Horrock's own paper. The *Tribune* had thus become the first newspaper with two official combat slots. "My breath was taken away," Mr. Rodrigue says. "I really sort of admired his balls for doing it."

For his part, Mr. Horrock insists that Mr. Rodrigue misinterpreted his remarks and says he resents any suggestion that he may have abused his job as print pool coordinator. "I'm really out there to win a story. I'm not there to win an election. I'd do exactly what I did again."

Colonel Mulvey and the other military coordinators of the Joint Information Bureau tried hard to walk the fine line necessary to avoid becoming embroiled in the media's intramural combat, but the print pool's intrigues sometimes pushed them over the edge.

For the final press pool created for the war, one that the Saudis would lead into the newly liberated Kuwait City, the Saudis were instructed to "lose" the Kuwait visa application form submitted by a *Chicago Tribune* reporter and substitute one filled out by Mr. Rodrigue.

"We unfucked him," was the way one officer, who asked to remain anonymous, described the military's resolution of the Rodrigue problem.

A footnote: Three days after the war, when Laurence A. Jolidon, a *USA Today* reporter, returned from the battlefield to Dhahran, he discovered that the office set up by the print pool was $20,000 in arrears. Mr. Jolidon, a former print pool coordinator, had worked harder than any of the rest of us to try and make the print pool work. Once the members of the print pool voted to set up an office in the hotel, it was Mr. Jolidon who volunteered to set it up. He signed for hotel space, and the copying and fax machines in our behalf.

Reporters for major news organizations, who had already paid the $600-a-month fee for running the office, chipped in again to help him pay off some of the creditors, but other members of the profession the military insisted on calling the "pencil people" left Dhahran without paying their bills. For them the war and its peculiar way of forcing journalists to acknowledge obligations to each other were just distant memories, if that.

"I thought we were all in this mess together," says Mr. Jolidon. "It never occurred to me that I was going to get stuck with the bill."

Chapter 5

Unilaterals: Risky Business

U.S. Marine Corps self-propelled howitzers roll across the desert. (U.S. Marine Corps)

Cats pranced on the tables in the kitchen of the Fao Hotel in Hafar al Batin and the stench of the raw sewage flowing in the street often seasoned the air in the dining room. It was a far cry from the elegant Dhahran International Hotel where the media pools were based, but it was home for Paul McEnroe and dozens of other unilateral reporters who decided the only way to get the news was to break the rules.

Mr. McEnroe, a reporter for the Minneapolis *Star-Tribune*, didn't have much time to probe the mystery of what was going on in the kitchen during dinner. That was when he had to keep one eye on the door leading in from the street.

The U.S. press had an agreement with the Pentagon that combat coverage would be carried out by journalists working in pools with media escorts. The Saudis had stiffened it with a decree that said any unescorted journalists found within 100 miles of the war zone would be arrested and deported. Hafar is about 60 miles south of the Iraqi border—well within the restricted zone.

The chief enforcer seemed to be this brawny, blond, crew-cut U.S. Army captain who often barged into the Fao at suppertime and arrested journalists. Mr. McEnroe—who later managed to get out to the cutting edge of combat, despite all the rules—was determined that the enforcer was not going to catch him. When things got hot in Hafar al Batin, he and a colleague went out and hid in the desert.

Unilaterals filled in some murky places in the picture of the Gulf War. They were the first to unravel the mystery of the fighting at Khafji, the first to show allied forces in action during the ground war, and they beat the media pool sent from Dhahran to cover the liberation of Kuwait City by a full day—an eternity in the age of electronic journalism.

But a study of the coverage of the war shows that, despite the life-risking chances that many of the unilaterals took, they could operate only at the fringes of this war. For the most part they could not answer the question that kept Americans glued to their television sets and devouring newspapers: What was going on in the battlefield? With few exceptions, the lead stories were drawn from pool reports or official briefings and not from unilaterals' accounts.

For his efforts, Mr. McEnroe was arrested twice, shot at, and nearly killed. "It was a great adventure, but I'd really have to think about doing it again like that, though. We were completely off bounds. We were way off the edge," says the reporter, who frequently worried about his four-year-old daughter when considering the risks he took in the desert.

Luck and the sudden collapse of the Iraqis saved him. "If the conflict had been less one-sided, there can be little doubt there would have been many casualties in the media," concludes David Beresford of the *Guardian*, a British newspaper, who was with Mr. McEnroe during his wild ride to Kuwait City.

Hafar al Batin became a base for many unilateral reporters during the final buildup for the ground war. It is a tiny desert crossroads town with a few seedy hotels and a handful of businesses, but the big military convoys from the south came up through it and soldiers from frontline units to the north of Hafar came down to buy things or just to get relief from the dirt and the monotony of waiting in the often clammy damp of the winter desert.

"We'd befriend the soldiers who would come in for a meal. We'd give them keys to our hotel room; that way they could have a hot shower and call home. Without even asking, they would just kinda talk about what was going on," recalls Mr. McEnroe.

He and a photographer would also go out to Egyptian army units. "We took pictures of them and brought them back the next day. We'd play messages for their wives over the phone and take tapes back to them and they loved it."

Mr. McEnroe learned enough from his research to break stories that Iraqi death squads were operating behind enemy lines, enforcing discipline, and that American and British special forces units were in Iraq, using lasers to designate targets for attack from the air.

But he was also preparing for a more ambitious project: to move with allied forces when the fighting started. For that he had to look military. He, Mr. Beresford, and two other journalists working with them had rented a four-wheel drive jeep similar to those used by military units. To make it even more similar they had smeared it with mud and marked it with an upside down *V*, using radar-reflecting tape—the official mark being used by allied units.

For $2,000 they bought camouflage uniforms, boots, chemical warfare suits, and flak jackets from enterprising soldiers they'd met from the U.S. 2d Armored Cavalry Regiment. "We'd meet them at night around the Fao Hotel. They'd toss this shit out of trucks and we'd pay them and they'd take off. It was like bad TV," says Mr. McEnroe.

One evening the reporter was chatting up a female Army MP he had met in a restaurant when the enforcer got him. "All of a sudden this outside middle linebacker type comes up and tells me I'm under arrest for talking about security matters to soldiers."

The enforcer, who identified himself simply as Army Capt. John R. Koko, then said he was going to fetch some other MPs to arrest Mr. McEnroe, who promptly hopped in his jeep and spent the night sleeping in the desert.

For Mr. McEnroe, who saw all of his expensive preparations going up in smoke, it was a frightening experience. For Captain Koko, who had spent the better part of two months struggling with the Army's VII Corps to set up a jury-rigged pool system that he knew would fail, rousting unilaterals was a kind of therapeutic release.

"Those people in Hafar had no limitations. I just felt it was unfair to the people in the pools who had agreed to play by the rules. They had so many constraints on them that I just felt I had to make it more difficult for the unilaterals. I was frustrated. At the time it seemed like the right thing to do," recalls the officer, who following the war resigned his Army commission.

Captain Koko generally sent European reporters back to Dhahran, but he let Americans go with a warning to return to Dhahran. Captain Koko was right about the unfairness of it all. It took days, sometimes weeks for pool journalists to get their products back to Dhahran. Even pool journalists with units operating within a few hours drive of Hafar al Batin ran into enormous obstacles. But Mr. McEnroe could fax his copy home from his seedy hotel within minutes.

When the war started, Mr. McEnroe swung his jeep into the baggage train behind his newly won friends in Egypt's 4th Tank Division. By Tuesday night, they were nearing Kuwait City Airport when they heard a BBC radio report that said a CBS television crew was already in Kuwait City, which seemed quiet.

At that point, Mr. Beresford insisted, "We've got to go. We've got to go." One of the four journalists was reluctant to leave the protection of the Egyptians, but Mr. Beresford and Mr. McEnroe finally won him over.

Getting directions from a U.S. Army Special Forces officer with the Egyptians, they struck out on their own with Mr. McEnroe driving and Mr. Beresford walking ahead of the jeep, looking for mines. They stumbled into a battle that was just ending. Iraqi tanks burned in the distance as menacing U.S. A-10 attack aircraft buzzed overhead. A group of Iraqi soldiers tried to surrender to them. Using sign language, the journalists told them to go back to their vehicles and sleep.

In the darkness, Mr. McEnroe could hear armored vehicles coming up behind them. Then he heard voices. They seemed to be Iraqi voices. The journalists abandoned the jeep and ran to a nearby fence. "I figured this is it. They've seen us and now they're coming," he recalls.

It was the crew of a Bradley Fighting Vehicle from the U.S. Tiger Brigade. Rifle-carrying infantry dismounted and began stalking toward the fence. "I just started shouting 'USA! Americans! Minnesota! Minnesota!' They were bellowing orders. 'Hands up! Walk slow!'"

The soldiers later explained that they had picked up the journalists using night-vision glasses from four miles away. "They said if we had gone 100 yards more, we would have been in their kill sack. Either tanks or the .50 caliber machine gun would have done it," says Mr. McEnroe.

After being detained until daylight, the four set off again for Kuwait City. A Marine unit at the airport fired a few machine gun bursts over them, but they made it into the city in time to see the bedlam of liberation. "Women in veils were trying to kiss us. Men were firing shots into the air."

Then they saw the crowd part as a Land Rover carrying a U.S. flag headed into the embassy compound. Inside it, Mr. McEnroe recognized an American reporter he knew who invited him to tag along.

But he didn't recognize the officer who was leading the group. "There's this big, tall, lanky guy strutting around. He looks at me and he goes, 'You and I will never witness the joy of freedom like this as long as we live again in our lifetime.' It was like music to him, all of this gunfire. I say this is terrific. Who is this guy? The reporters look at me like where have you been."

It was the Marines' commander, Lt. Gen. Walter E. Boomer, leading a group of reporters from one of the Marine pools.

Down the street, a CBS camera crew was set up so that it could shoot against the backdrop of Kuwait City's distinctive towers. To them, what excited Mr. McEnroe and General Boomer was very old news by then. They had been feeding live broadcasts, via satellite, for 20 hours.

They were the winner of the unofficial, but desperate, race to be the first journalists to enter Kuwait City. For Mr. McEnroe and his group getting there had been a dangerous adventure, a memorable feature story. For David Green, 47, a freelance producer-cameraman with a contract to work for CBS, getting to places first in wartime is his business.

Mr. Green and his sound man, Andy Thompson, both Englishmen, are expert navigators. They had covered wars in Vietnam, the Middle East, Africa, and El Salvador. "If you cover wars," explains Mr. Green, "there's a window. If you can get ahead of the MPs it's fat city. There's plenty of war to cover. But if you get bogged down, you're stuck with all the bureaucrats. We were not about to do that."

Getting the first visual of a liberated Kuwait City meant millions for the television networks battling for ratings in the Gulf War. Mr. Green's entourage, which included three Land Rovers, probably approached a million dollars worth of investment. "We had state-of-the-art equipment, seven boxes weighing about a ton. We had three generators, two satellite phones, two LORANs [navigation devices]. We had enough gas and enough water for from ten days to two weeks," recalls Mr. Green. "If we had gone over a mine, they would have seen us for a long time."

There were three other networks in the running. "We tried for a long time to live within pool rules against unilateral reporting," explains Terry Frieden, who coordinated CNN's crews. "By the second day of the ground war, we felt we simply couldn't wait any longer for the Saudis or the U.S. to give us the go-ahead to move our satellite dish and transmission facilities into Kuwait. We went on our own."

The CNN crew headed toward the border just behind Mr. Green's CBS unit early Monday morning. About three miles into Kuwait, Mr. Green recalls being confronted by an American major, who explained that the MPs had stopped a CNN crew on the border and were now looking for a CBS crew that, they had been told, was just ahead.

The CBS crew members, who were wearing camouflage uniforms and British chemical warfare suits, told the major they hadn't seen any CBS crew. In his crisp British accent, Mr. Green explained that they were an ITN crew operating under the authority of Kuwait's crown prince. "We told him we were going back," recalls Mr. Green, "but of course we didn't. We headed straight up the road. Once you have an edge, you're not going to give it up."

Meanwhile, the real ITN crew, headed by correspondent Sandy Gall, had been busted by the Saudi Information Ministry. Mr. Gall had scooped the world by showing Saudi troops invading Kuwait. Afterward, the Saudis had warned them not to shoot their cameras again without permission.

"However when we defied the rules again," Mr. Gall later explained in a discussion of the war published by Britain's International Press Institute, "the men from the ministry became extremely shirty and took our passes away, turning a deaf ear to my plea that we were merely doing our job of informing the world and that we were, damn it all, Allies."[1]

The final entry in the great unilateral race for Kuwait City was Forrest Sawyer of ABC, but on Monday his situation looked hopeless. His first mistake was to set himself up for the wrong war. As many of us believed, Mr. Sawyer was sure there would be heavy fighting and perhaps the use of chemical weapons at the much-publicized Saddam Wall, the network of sand berms, mine fields, and oil-filled trenches that Iraqi forces had built along Kuwait's southern border.

Through weeks of behind-the-scenes negotiations, Mr. Sawyer had persuaded Saudi military officials to allow his crew and his four-truck convoy of television satellite broadcasting equipment to cross the border with Saudi forces at a point in western Kuwait where the Saudi commanders expected the most fighting.

But the big battles never materialized, and early Monday, as Saudi forces inched through the Saddam Wall, taking ample time for tea breaks and prayers, Mr. Sawyer realized he was in the wrong place. "I said I've got to get to Kuwait City. This whole thing [the war] is falling apart."

His problem was that his convoy was also falling apart. First the truck carrying a generator had a flat tire with no spare. Next the big six-wheel truck carrying the satellite dish was given a refueling of gasoline mixed with sand that destroyed its engine. Mr. Sawyer raced back to Hafar al Batin where, after hours of frantic bargaining, he convinced the Saudi owner of a baby diaper service to rent him another truck.

ABC then roared east, finally hitting the coastal road leading to Kuwait City. While the frequent roadblocks there had been an obstacle for the other networks' crews, Mr. Sawyer's team, which looked very military—with the exception of the diaper truck—whizzed through them all waving a pass from a Saudi prince.

But they were still hours behind CBS's David Green who had been out in front, exploring his "window" on the war. On Monday, the CBS unit followed a Saudi tank column that frequently stalled and finally stopped. Then Mr. Green moved on ahead of it and started to videotape a burning house. That was a mistake. "The Iraqis were still in there and they started firing with small arms on us. It turned out the whole stretch of road behind us hadn't been cleared yet," recalls Mr. Green.

As they fled, the crew saw Marine Harrier jets strafing Iraqi tanks. They pulled up on a rise a half mile away and fired up the generators for a live broadcast on CBS morning news. Arranging a satellite hookup from the desert is a risky, time-consuming business. First, Mr. Green called CBS on his satellite phone, "which puts a hell of a beacon up there for an AWACs [the U.S. Airborne Warning and Control aircraft] to see."

"Then you go through a whole 10-minute rigmarole. You call New York and they call around the world." Finally the crew's portable satellite dish was linked up to the correct satellite, and the CBS crew's correspondent, Bob McKeown, was on the air, narrating the action under way on the battlefield around them.

The crew "came up" on the satellite again for the evening news and then struggled out of their sleeping bags at dawn on Tuesday morning for a CBS special midnight show. "Once you come up, everybody and his brother wants to talk to you," recalls Mr. Green, who was becoming edgy because the front had moved on.

By mid-afternoon, the CBS crew had passed more long columns of Saudi tanks and hit a four-lane highway. They were less than 20 miles from Kuwait City and were following two American HMMVs (the successor to the Army jeep). The HMMVs seemed to know where they were going, but then they did an abrupt U-turn and disappeared.

Mr. Green approached a Saudi tank crew, who indicated in broken English that it was safe to go into Kuwait City. "We were not sure they understood the question but took a chance and went ahead." Then they met a Kuwaiti civilian who said the Iraqis had evacuated.

It was 4:45 P.M. The CBS crew, racing to catch the last available daylight, made it into the city and were "firing up" near the U.S. embassy at 6 P.M. when, as if on cue, a menacing-looking group of young men carrying rifles approached. They were Kuwaiti resistance fighters and they got on live.

It was time for the daily U.S. military briefing from Riyadh. Officials there were asked whether Kuwait City was liberated. They couldn't confirm it. CBS switched from that to their man McKeown, standing coolly in downtown Kuwait. He confirmed it.

Still, it was eerie. By 7:30 P.M., the crowd around Mr. Green's vehicles dissolved and the streets were almost totally empty. CBS may have confirmed that the city was safe, but the Kuwaitis had yet to be convinced. A U.S. Marine unit came by to secure the embassy and warned Mr. Green that he wasn't safe, but the CBS unit broadcast through the night. Australian television wanted an interview, then Japanese television.

Mr. Sawyer's ABC crew rolled into the pitch dark city just before midnight. He knocked on the only door he could find that had a light. It turned out to a hideout for six refugee families who, seeing the ABC crew's military uniforms and flak jackets, started singing and dancing and crying. They had been liberated.

For Mr. Sawyer, it wasn't time to dance, yet. He wasn't convinced the Iraqis had left town and wanted a place to put up his dish that would be safe from sniper fire. Just then a white BMW carrying two men brandishing Uzis showed up. They were Kuwaiti resistance leaders. ABC had found the perfect base for a series of stories Mr. Sawyer later filed on the Kuwaiti resistance effort. His satellite dish was mounted on the roof of their headquarters.

By Wednesday morning, when the real dancing and singing and celebratory shooting got under way, both crews had already broadcast hours and hours of the story of the liberation of Kuwait City. They were exhausted.

The official press pool from Dhahran, organized by the Saudis and the JIB, didn't arrive until Wednesday evening. Mr. Green recalls that he wasn't really overjoyed to see them.

"The guys up in the front are great. It's when you get to the JIB guys that you get in trouble."

Note

[1]Peter Preston, comp., *Reporting the War: A Collection of Experiences and Reflections on the Gulf* (London: British Executive of the International Press Institute, 1991).

Chapter 6

The Future: War with No Witnesses?

Secretary of Defense Dick Cheney talks with reporters in Saudi Arabia on August 23, 1990. Behind him to his right is Assistant Secretary of Defense for Public Affairs Pete Williams. (U.S. Marine Corps)

In all American wars, the number of journalists who actually witness the violence, danger, bloodshed, and the snafus of combat is a tiny minority of those who go to cover the war.

This phenomenon continues to amaze the military. Colonel Mulvey, who fended off the crowds of reporters at the JIB in the Dhahran International Hotel, recalls that as the commander of a rifle platoon in Vietnam, "I never saw a reporter during the entire year in the field."

In the Gulf War, as in Vietnam, most of the coverage came from reporters in hotels. One difference was that the plush hotels in Riyadh and Dhahran, where some 1,600 journalists worked, lacked bars. Another difference was that the military had found ways to make the hotel warrior's life much easier. Televised briefings, the pool reports, and CNN all provided the heightened illusion of being near the war.

For the 10 percent of us who went out to the field, though, we discovered that the military had also found ways to make working conditions there more difficult. We encountered multiple layers of control, at least one of which always seemed to be there. Barriers seemed to raise automatically to blur the reality; buffers were always at the ready to blunt the sharp edges of truth.

For American troops, the single most violent event of the war was on Monday, February 25. It was an Iraqi Scud missile whose engine spluttered and died, sending it into an arc that brought it crashing through the corrugated metal roof of a warehouse near Dhahran that was in use as a barracks. A blinding fireball rose over the building and shock waves sent a spray of shrapnel into sleeping bodies. Twenty-seven GIs were killed and 98 were injured.

This didn't happen along the front lines; it happened in the rear, 2.7 miles from the Dhahran International Hotel where the military's JIB formed the pools of reporters that were supposed to be the public's primary mechanism for learning about this war.

Scott Applewhite, an Associated Press photographer, was in the parking lot of the hotel when he heard there had been an explosion. He and a reporter instinctively jumped in a car. Finding the site was not hard at all. Medevac helicopters hovered over the smoke-spewing wreckage like bees carrying searchlights.

Getting in was difficult. A line of MPs blocked the front of the building. Mr. Applewhite found a Saudi policeman who escorted him around to the rear. Picking his way through the debris, the photographer entered the building. He took a picture of some empty sleeping bags lying amid the clutter. A British soldier approached, shouting at him: "You bloody fuck!" Mr. Applewhite took the soldier's picture and then quickly left the building.

"I didn't want to attract a whole lot of attention. I wanted to get out there where they were evacuating people and that's where I got nailed." The military had spent hours showing U.S. reporters how quickly they can handle casualties. Mr. Applewhite had even been to one prewar press event on a hospital ship where journalists were invited to shoot pictures of volunteer "casualties" covered with ketchup to enhance the drama.

But when he came near the real thing—as real as this war got—15 U.S. and Saudi military police officers descended upon him. He was handcuffed, beaten, and had one of his cameras smashed as he stood his ground, insisting he was an accredited U.S. journalist and had every right to be there.

They demanded his film, and he gave them a roll, quietly substituting an empty roll and pushing the real one down his pant leg. It was a symbolic gesture: he hadn't taken any meaningful pictures yet, and he was not about to. Mr. Applewhite was led out of the compound. He saw a U.S. officer standing in the crowd and asked him why the press was being barred.

"Host-nation sensitivities," replied the officer. Then Mr. Applewhite saw a Catholic priest walk past the MPs and the Saudis into the building. Then he saw a Saudi prince, the deputy governor of Saudi Arabia's Eastern Province, driving through the cordon. Mr. Applewhite knew him.

"I said, 'Hey, I've got to get in there.'" The Saudi official saw no problem and waved Mr. Applewhite into the car, but the American MPs chased him and forced him to get back out. Then Mr. Applewhite saw what he thought was his salvation: an Army major who had arrived from the JIB.

"I said we have got to get a pool organized. This is an historic event. If we don't get in now, there'll be nothing to get." The major said he was not authorized to do that. Well, Mr. Applewhite pleaded, could he escort one photographer in there?

The major looked at Mr. Applewhite. "He says, 'I'm here to escort you out.'"

For a couple of fleeting moments, the AP photographer had broken through the invisible barrier, a kind of plastic bag or cocoon of controls that the military preferred to keep around reporters in this war. While some of us managed to get out of the hotels, most of us never escaped the cocoon.

Officially sanctioned censorship was rarely present. Of the 1,300 reports by reporters working in pools, only one was officially censored by the Pentagon. What got into those reports, however, was heavily influenced by access. Publication of the reports was seriously influenced by delay.

Unofficially, the cocoon was everywhere. "I never saw any organized efforts at censorship," recalls Lt. Charles E. Hoskinson, Jr., a 29-year-old reservist who served as a pool escort. "All I saw was the natural tendency in the military to keep things under control."

Mr. Hoskinson, who is a newspaper reporter in civilian life, says that when journalists behaved irresponsibly, such as barging into the living quarters of off-duty troops, the controls were enhanced. They were also enhanced when reporters saw something that might endanger the career of a commander.

Steve Elfers, an *Army Times* photographer, recalls riding on a patrol with a 1st Cavalry unit shortly after midnight on February 4. The air war was three weeks old, and U.S. fighter-bombers approaching the border looked like clouds of fireflies before they flicked off their running lights. Flights of B-52s, whose missions and effects remain unexplained, created a vague rumbling sound in the distance.

The patrol heard on the radio that an American soldier, lying next to a truck carrying a ground surveillance radar, had been hit.

Mr. Elfers and an accompanying reporter asked to see the site. Although it had initially been described as an enemy mortar attack, it soon became obvious to the group of soldiers and the two reporters examining the debris that the soldier had probably been hit by a U.S. Air Force antiradiation missile. There had been no Iraqi mortars in the area and whatever had hit the truck had hit it dead center with one shot.

There was an ominous silence as Mr. Elfers continued to snap pictures of the radar, similar to Iraqi units that had been under attack by the U.S. Air Force. Then the executive officer of the cavalry regiment came up and said they had to go, some Iraqi prisoners had been captured nearby.

They left, but it was a ruse. There were no enemy prisoners. Then the unit's public affairs officer asked Mr. Elfers to turn over his film. The photographer refused, insisting that it be given to the press pool courier. "I figure if they tried to flag [censor] the film, fine. I didn't think I had any problem because I had shot the radar at an angle that would obscure the design."

After a great deal of back and forth, including at least one phone call to the 1st Cavalry Division's commander, Maj. Gen. John H. Tilelli, Mr. Elfers agreed to drive back to the Army VII Corps rear and to hand the film personally to the corps's top public affairs officer, Lt. Col. James W. Gleisberg. He remembers meeting Lieutenant Colonel Gleisberg—a personage whom other journalists working with units in the corps rarely saw—waiting at a roadside filling station to pick up the film.

Two days later, when Mr. Elfers discovered the film hadn't arrived back in Dhahran, he called Lt. Col. Gleisberg, who, according to Mr. Elfers, said he had forgotten to give it to the courier. The film, and a story describing the presumed friendly fire incident made it back to Dhahran four days after the event.

"Basically I think they sat on it for at least 24 hours to kill its news value," believes Mr. Elfers. "Friendly fire was kind of a hot topic at that time."

Shortly before the ground war, Army Apache helicopter pilots had shown John Balzar, a *Los Angeles Times* reporter, videotapes from the helicopter's cameras showing Iraqi soldiers being mowed down by the gunship's Gatling gun. When Mr. Balzar wrote about it, television networks wanted the tapes. Then the Army decided they shouldn't have been released at all. What they had shown was too real.

After that, the lid came down on coverage of the Apaches. An hour after the cease-fire, Mr. Balzar asked Col. Emmitt Gibson, commander of an Apache brigade, what the night-flying Apaches had done to the fleeing Republican Guard units during the last night of the war. "Do you have a security clearance?" was the colonel's acid reply.

"People still ask me, 'so what, did we miss anything?'" says Mr. Balzar. "I say to them I don't know." When he finally examined the Apache unit, after the war had ended, many of the helicopters were grounded. The explanation was that they had outrun their fuel supply. "The other possibility," recalls Mr. Balzar, "is that many of the Apaches weren't working. I'll never know."

Peter Van Sant, a CBS correspondent, discovered the walls of the cocoon when his crew kept pressing Marine commanders to get them up front with a reconnaissance unit where they could record some of the action. "They would never let us do that," he recalls. "There was a feeling on the battlefield that they didn't want to be the unit that had the reporters killed."

The matter of how the press covers the next war involving American forces is an issue that is too important to be left to the press or the military to decide, but, in a vacuum, they will decide it. Wars are not bus crashes. They live in history books for thousands of years. War heroes, or politicians who have packaged themselves as such (Presidents Eisenhower, Kennedy, and Bush), have dominated much of this nation's politics over the past 40 years.

The hard lessons of war must be learned, not reshaped to fit commanders' predictions. The matter of what worked and what didn't in the Gulf War battlefields will cost taxpayers hundreds of billions of dollars and drive major federal budget decisions for years to come. This was a war where the military remained in control of most of the evidence and where the

Army commanders' paranoid fear of the media helped bury one of the most positive Army stories since World War II. The acceptance of a loss like that raises the deeper issue of whether the Army becomes more open or closed to public view. If it is ignored, the question of an increasingly inward-looking Army is one that could come back some day to haunt us all.

It is difficult for most of who us who witnessed the swift-moving nature of this war and experienced the chaos on the battlefield to see how it could have been covered without some sort of pool mechanism that guaranteed access to commanders, their units, and their communications systems. "I've got to have that access," says Mr. Applewhite, the AP photographer. "I've got to be able to use their vehicles, their helicopters."

"If I was faced with an actual choice, to join the pool or play solitaire, I would accept the pool," says Juan O. Tamayo, a reporter for the *Miami Herald*. "Imagine the chaos if we had not had a pool system. Half the press corps would have been out looking for glory with the Marines and the 82d Airborne. And the 1st Infantry [Division], which fought a lot, would have had to beg for coverage. Would such disorganized reports have given us an accurate view of the war? I doubt it."

Yet the dominant voices in the media's internal debate over this matter come from the Washington bureau chiefs. "To those who argue that if the DOD pool is dismantled we might miss some major news event, I reply that we missed major news events when we were in the pool—namely, important parts of the Persian Gulf reflagging operation, the invasion of Panama, and most of the Gulf War," argues Stan Cloud, who heads *Time* magazine's Washington bureau.

"I think from what I know of it that when the ground war began, it would have been perfectly reasonable for groups of reporters in four-wheel-drive vehicles, assuming they had communications, to cover that war with no difficulty at all. Of course they would have to exercise self-censorship," says Andrew J. Glass, Washington bureau chief for Cox Newspapers, who spent most of the war covering press briefings at the Hyatt Regency Hotel in Riyadh.

To the hundreds of journalists who espouse what is known as the drive-up theory of covering future wars, the Marines have a word. "That's bullshit," says General Boomer, the war's most astute handler of the media.

"You cannot have people wandering around on the battlefield on their own. It's not fair to the soldiers. You can say, well we'll take care of our own, but you can't. The Marines will wind up having to provide protection and in combat we don't have time to do that."

To make future pool systems work, according to General Boomer and other military officials who have thought about it, the American press will have to do something that has been, until now, unthinkable: It will have to agree on an upper limit to the numbers of reporters covering combat. That would mean quotas. That would mean some media outlets would cover combat and others would not.

Colonel Mulvey, the Army officer who headed the JIB in Dhahran, offers a quid pro quo that will be difficult for both the Army and the press to achieve. "We owe you a better attitude among the commanders to support you on the battlefield, but the media has to work on [limitations on] the numbers."

That's not all the military wants. General Boomer wants the reporters who do reach the field to have some experience in covering military matters. That was not often the case in this war, where the regulars who cover the Pentagon stayed there, while less experienced reporters were sent to Dhahran. As the draft, which once gave most reporters a rough education in the military, fades deeper into history, this problem will only get worse.

"It shouldn't be amateur night at the follies as far as combat correspondents are concerned," argues the Marine general, who has found some reporters who agree with him. Ed Offley, a *Seattle Post-Intelligencer* reporter who has specialized in defense matters for 10 years, believes that part of the cocoon problem relates to reporters he saw "who were totally bewildered and lost in an alien military environment."

"Thus their stories tended to reflect a surface impression of the events at hand, and their attempts to obtain news were easily diverted and manipulated by military PAO [public affairs] officers who—it must be said—know far more about how the press functions than these disoriented journalists knew about the war they were trying to cover."

To say that the military has the most public support up to this point in this ongoing debate would seem to be an understatement. Polls taken by the Gallup Organization and Princeton Survey Research in January 1991 show a substantial majority of Americans felt that the media's coverage made it "harder" for U.S. officials to prosecute the war. Americans also felt that the press was not overly controlled by the military.

Asked whether they supported military censorship, a stunning 79 percent said they thought it was a "good idea."

And that is just the entranceway to the pit the media dug for themselves in the Gulf. While war correspondents as far back as the Civil War have generally tended to be admired figures, in this war they were lampooned on "Saturday Night Live" for their often farcical questions posed to military briefers in Riyadh.

Henry Allen, a Vietnam veteran and feature writer for the *Washington Post*, said the briefings "are making reporters look like fools, nitpickers, and egomaniacs, like dilettantes who have spent exactly none of their lives on the end of a gun or even a shovel; dinner party commandos, slouching inquisitors, collegiate spitball artists—people who have never been in a fistfight much less combat; a whining, self-righteous, upper middle class mob."

Evolving technology offers the military yet another argument to tighten controls on the press. Within a few years, the hand-carried satellite phone will be a reality, providing the possibility for instantaneous coverage of the battlefield. "That's a tough issue," says General Boomer. "We worry about the enemy seeing in real time what we're doing."

"Say you had 12 uplinks running around on the battlefield. The enemy would pick up live pictures and say, 'Aha.' It's a tough situation. I don't think the question here is as one-sided as some of our people seem to think," says Walter Porges, vice president of news practices for ABC.

Where do we go from here? Perhaps nowhere. The military's hardened attitude toward the press has persisted since Grenada, despite repeated attempts by Pentagon civilians to paper it over. There seems to be moderate-to-strong support in the media for sticking to what guns we have, insisting on the right to unilateral coverage at any price. Dick Cheney, the secretary of defense, has shown no tendency thus far to compromise other than to say he is "keeping an open mind."

One upshot could be a reversion to Grenada: a war without witnesses. It would be a comfort to some; we could all learn what happened at the same televised briefing. Leaving an increasingly elite military force with total control over information, however, would be a dark day for those who can recall that the point of national security is to protect a democracy.

It seems that the first thing the media must do to move the military is to develop a position that seems reasonable to the public at large. While it would disappoint the absolutists among us, it would attract support from the legal and academic communities, which, up to now, have simply been watching the press and the Pentagon go at each other.

The British experience in the Gulf is worth studying. The military and the media in that country followed a plan worked out after the Falklands War entitled, "Proposed Working Arrangements in Time of Tension and War."

It would have saved us months of arguing in Dhahran, for the agreement forced the press lords to determine in advance who would cover a fixed number of combat slots provided by the military. "That was a very tedious process which the newspapers got very cross about," recalls Peter Preston, editor of the *Guardian*.

The newspaper publishers' association drew names out of a hat and then settled down to what Mr. Preston calls "a sensible sorting out and haggling." The *Guardian*'s correspondent, for example, wasn't chosen, but Mr. Preston got the London *Observer*'s reporter to give up his place in return for the *Guardian*'s daily copy.

In return for a limit on the number of journalists, the British military agreed to allow satellite phones and satellite broadcasting equipment in the field, enabling British reporters to get their copy back to London more quickly, beating the American pony express system by days or, in some cases, weeks. It wasn't perfect, notes Mike Jeremy, foreign news editor of London's Independent Television Network (ITN). "There were frustrations because it [the satellite dish] was moving a lot and it wasn't usable while it was moving." But while American reporters with U.S. armored units in northern Kuwait and Iraq had no way to communicate, their British counterparts had a dish that followed the British 1st Armored Division through Iraq and then went to Kuwait City.

"We knew the entire battle plan a week before the land war started," recalls Colin Wills of London's *Sunday Mirror*. "On a professional level, needless to say, it was very frustrating. To be in the know and not be able to file a word was like being given the secret of alchemy and at that same instant being struck dumb. But that kind of censorship was vital for the success of the operation and for saving lives, and nobody begrudged it."

Patrick Bishop of the *Daily Telegraph*, one of the few British reporters permitted in the U.S. pools, covered the Marines.

After that, he became a unilateral reporter operating out of Hafar al Batin, an experience that he vastly preferred. He sees the dilemma ahead.

"For the military, pools seem to be the only option when it comes to controlling the media. After the latest experience, I doubt whether they will get many takers next time there is a war."

There will never be peace in the media over this issue, just as there was never peace among us at the Dhahran International Hotel. In this war, there was always one more bizarre media scene ready to be played out.

Terry Frieden, who coordinated CNN's television crews in Dhahran, recalls the morning when Charles Jaco, the network's chief Scud watcher, was standing before the camera behind the hotel, near what had been a putting green. He was narrating as he watched a Scud being hit by a Patriot missile. It was right over the hotel, but he followed the censorship rules, which forbade disclosing the location.

Then he sensed this strange smell. Screaming, "Gas!" the correspondent dove for his gas mask. It turned out to be methane from an oil tank farm across the street.

This phony gas attack galvanized audiences around the world, illustrating the risks of live coverage. It also demonstrated some of the dangers lurking for war correspondents. *Newsweek*'s answer to the problem of how to escape the cocoon in this war was hiring retired Col. David H. Hackworth, the most decorated veteran of the Vietnam War.

While the rest of us slaved compliantly in specific pools out in the field during the windup to the air war, Mr. Hackworth moved from division to division like a wraith, relying on a network of officer cronies to float through the controls. After the Jaco incident, he and Mr. Jaco met in CNN's studio at the Dhahran International. Just moments before they were to appear, live, on the "Larry King Show," Mr. Hackworth lunged at Mr. Jaco's throat and threatened to punch him.

"You're scaring my kids!" shouted Mr. Hackworth. "I don't like you scaring my kids!" Mr. Jaco refused to go on the show. Mr. Frieden grabbed the phone and called CNN headquarters in Atlanta. "I said, 'I don't know if you should put Mr. Hackworth on.'"

But in a war where reporters often donned soldiers' camouflage uniforms to tell their stories, Mr. Hackworth had no trouble at all shifting to his guise as a reporter to tell his. He smiled sweetly, Mr. Frieden recalls, and then he said, "We're not going to attack that country [Iraq] until we turn it into a waffle."

It was a most peculiar war. Except to Mr. Applewhite of the Associated Press, it revealed little of its violence. There were also moments of nobility. On Thursday, a few hours after President Bush had declared the end of the combat, I saw GIs stripping off their protective chemical suits and giving them to thinly clad members of Saddam Hussein's elite Republican Guards as they squatted, shivering in their barbed-wire compounds.

But few of us saw much in the way of nobility in the hotels. I remember one cameraman who planted himself on the stairway of the Dhahran International Hotel early in the air war. It was one of the first Scud alerts, and he was partially blocking the streams of journalists racing to get to the air raid shelters in the basement.

"Hey, you're in the way," said one reporter, who pushed him aside. "You asshole," snarled the cameraman, who shoved back. "I'll get you for that."

When I was sitting on the basement floor after that, trying to concentrate on a book through the filmy lenses of my cheap, Soviet-made gas mask, a radio reporter behind me began narrating what was happening. "We are sitting here in Dhahran as at least four Scud missiles are approaching," he announced, breathlessly, through one of the few phones in the basement shelter area, primarily a kitchen used by the hotel.

How did he know what was happening? I wondered, as he stuck his microphone in front of the air-raid siren to give listeners a sample of its bansheelike howling. Then I heard it. Boom. Boom. Boom. There seemed to be several muffled explosions in the vicinity of the hotel.

There were more booms. As the radio reporter's hair-raising narration continued, I began worrying that my wife would be listening. She would be terrified, but all that I could tell her for sure was that there were a bunch of us sitting in a kitchen wearing these masks that made us look like giant insects. None of the Scuds hit Dhahran that night.

Later I decided that the reporter was guessing at the numbers of approaching Scuds by counting the booms, which were actually made by nearby Patriot missile batteries. They launched several missiles at each incoming target.

Much later, as most of us were packing our bags to go home, I discovered the real source of the booms. Our kitchen-shelter was located under a large walk-in cooler serving a hotel restaurant on the floor above. Several times an hour the restaurant workers went in there, slamming the heavy door behind them. The noise reverberated through the floor below: Boom. Boom. Boom.

In retrospect, it seems funny. But, for a number of American radio listeners that night, the real war was the Dhahran International Hotel's cooler door. They deserved better than that.

Chronology

Aug. 2, 1990 (Thurs.) Iraq invades Kuwait; President Bush orders economic sanctions against Iraq.

Aug. 7 (Tues.) First U.S. troops leave for Saudi Arabia; no reporters accompany them.

Aug. 12 (Sun.) Department of Defense National Media Pool, with 17 members, deployed. Journalists arrive in Dhahran, Saudi Arabia, on Aug. 13, accompanied by six military press officers, who establish Joint Information Bureau (JIB) in Dhahran International Hotel.

Aug. 16 (Thurs.) Of eight reporters who accompany Defense Secretary Dick Cheney to Middle East, four choose to stay on in Saudi Arabia, including *Washington Post* reporter Molly Moore.

Aug. 26 (Sun.) National Media Pool dissolved; there are now over 300 U.S. and foreign reporters in Saudi Arabia.

Aug. 29 (Wed.) Reporters in Saudi Arabia hold formal meeting to discuss creation of pools after Navy Capt. Mike Sherman—head of the JIB—announces that coverage will be done in pools.

Oct. 6 (Sat.) Pentagon sends a joint public affairs team to Saudi Arabia to prepare for media coverage of potential hostilities.

Nov. 8 (Thurs.) In a press conference, President Bush discusses decision to double number of U.S. troops in Saudi Arabia.

Dec. 14 (Fri.) Assistant Secretary of Defense for Public Affairs Pete Williams sends Washington, D.C., news executives a draft

Compiled by Mark Miller and Deborah Kalb of the Media Studies Project of his media coverage proposals. The plans call for sending 120 additional media personnel to Saudi Arabia at the start of hostilities, spell out pool arrangements, and discuss the military security review procedure. News executives object to Williams's proposal.

Jan. 7, 1991 (Mon.) Revised ground rules announced by Pentagon still not satisfactory to many of the news executives.

Jan. 15 (Tues.) Pentagon announces final revised version of ground rules and guidelines for press coverage in Gulf. Ground rules contain 12 categories of information that cannot be reported. Guidelines call for mandatory pool coverage.

Jan. 15–16 (Tues.–Wed.) United Nations deadline for Saddam Hussein to withdraw from Kuwait expires at midnight EST.

Jan. 16 (Wed.) Just after 6:30 P.M. EST, first reports appear on networks of air attacks on Baghdad. Press pools officially go into action.

Jan. 17 (Thurs.) Pentagon-chartered media plane arrives in Dhahran, Saudi Arabia, carrying 126 members of the press.

Jan. 19 (Sat.) Iraq orders all foreign journalists out of country; only Peter Arnett and his CNN crew and some Jordanian reporters are permitted to remain.

Jan. 21 (Mon.) Pete Williams announces Department of Defense ban on media covering return of U.S. casualties at Dover Air Force base in Delaware.

Jan. 23 (Wed.) White House Press Secretary Marlin Fitzwater criticizes CNN for Peter Arnett's report on his visit to what Iraqis describe as a baby-milk factory, bombed by U.S. planes.

Jan. 24 (Thurs.) CBS reports that correspondent Bob Simon and crew are missing. The four journalists had been taken prisoner by the Iraqis near the Saudi-Kuwait border, and were released on Mar. 2.

Jan. 29 (Tues.) CNN airs Peter Arnett's interview with Saddam Hussein. President Bush delivers State of the Union message.

Jan. 30 (Wed.) Eleven Marines are first U.S. soldiers killed in ground fighting west of Saudi border town of Khafji; Iraq had invaded Khafji Jan. 29.

Jan. 31 (Thurs.) Allies drive Iraqis out of Khafji; unilateral reporters get to scene before press pools; all networks use NBC correspondent Brad Willis's pool report.

Times-Mirror's "The People, the Press, and the War in the Gulf" report, based on polls taken Jan. 25–27, finds that eight in ten Americans give the press a positive rating for its war coverage. The report also concludes that 78 percent of Americans say the military is telling as much as it can about the war and that 72 percent believe the news organizations are trying to give an objective picture of the war.

Feb. 4 (Mon.) *Los Angeles Times* reporter Douglas Jehl sends memo to Col. William Mulvey, wartime JIB director, protesting military's cutting him off from various sources of information after he has written a controversial story.

Twenty-one House members sign letter to CNN President Tom Johnson complaining about Peter Arnett's coverage from Baghdad.

Feb. 12 (Tues.) Central Command Public Affairs Officer Capt. Ron Wildermuth announces military is doubling number of pools assigned to ground forces.

Feb. 13 (Wed.) U.S. Stealth fighter bombers kill Iraqi civilians in what Iraq claims was civilian shelter; U.S. claims structure was military command bunker.

Feb. 20 (Wed.) Senate Governmental Affairs Committee holds hearing on "Pentagon Rules on Media Access to the Persian Gulf War."

Feb. 23 (Sat.) Ground war begins, 8 P.M. EST; Cheney suspends briefings for half a day, until reports of early success in ground campaign.

Feb. 25 (Mon.) Debris from an Iraqi Scud missile hits barracks in Saudi Arabia, killing U.S. soldiers.

Feb. 26 (Tues.) CBS reporter Bob McKeown and his crew produce first live pictures from Kuwait City, having defied pool system.

Feb. 27 (Wed.) Gen. H. Norman Schwarzkopf's briefing on ground war televised live.

Feb. 28 (Thurs.) End of ground war; Iraq agrees to meet with U.S. to discuss cease-fire terms.

Mar. 25 (Mon.) A Times-Mirror study finds that eight in ten Americans approved of the news coverage of the war. Forty-five percent rate the coverage as excellent, as compared to 36 percent in January.

Apr. 15 (Mon.) Fifteen Washington, D.C., bureau chiefs meet at ABC to discuss pools and media coverage of war.

Apr. 29 (Mon.) The bureau chiefs send letter to Defense Secretary Cheney requesting meeting to talk about military-media relations. Bureau chiefs state that they are not in favor of repeating the Desert Storm–style pool system in future.

June 25 (Tues.) Following the bureau chiefs' lead, 17 top news executives send letter to Cheney. Enclosed with the letter is a report prepared by the bureau chiefs, spelling out various problems with the pool system.

Sept. 12 (Thurs.) Cheney meets with group of news executives to discuss coverage; he defends both the restrictions and the resulting coverage.

The Woodrow Wilson International Center for Scholars

The Center is the "living memorial" of the United States of America to the nation's twenty-eighth president, Woodrow Wilson. The U.S. Congress established the Woodrow Wilson Center in 1968 as an international institute for advanced study, "symbolizing and strengthening the fruitful relationship between the world of learning and the world of public affairs." The Center opened in 1970 under its own presidentially appointed board of directors.

Woodrow Wilson Center Special Studies

The work of the Center's Fellows, Guest Scholars, and staff and presentations and discussions at the Center's conferences, seminars, and colloquia often deserve timely circulation as contributions to public understanding of issues of national and international importance. The Woodrow Wilson Center Special Studies series is intended to make such materials available to interested scholars, practitioners, and other readers. In all its activities, the Woodrow Wilson Center is a nonprofit, nonpartisan organization, supported financially by annual appropriations from the U.S. Congress, and by the contributions of foundations, corporations, and individuals. Conclusions or opinions expressed in Center publications and programs are those of the authors and speakers and do not necessarily reflect the views of the Center's staff, Fellows, Trustees, advisory groups, or any individuals or organizations that provide financial support to the Center.

The Media Studies Project

Lawrence W. Lichty, Director

Advisory Council

Peter Braestrup, Chairman; Philip S. Cook, Vice Chairman; Leo Bogart; Alan Brinkley; William H. Chafe

The Media Studies Project of the Woodrow Wilson International Center for Scholars was established in 1988 to encourage scholarly research on the role of the media in American life. The Project conducts research and writing on a broad spectrum of the media, including electronic media, newspapers, film, magazines, and books, but with a special emphasis on news. The Project sponsors Guest Scholars, and holds conferences and seminars on media-related topics.

Support for the Media Studies Project's analysis of the coverage of the Gulf War has been granted by the Lynde and Harry Bradley Foundation and the John M. Olin Foundation. Additional funding for the Media Studies Project has been received from the Ford Foundation, the Horace W. Goldsmith Foundation, the Greentree Foundation, the Sarah Scaife Foundation, the J.M. Foundation, the William H. Donner Foundation, and the Earhart Foundation.

Publications of the Media Studies Project
Books
Published by the Woodrow Wilson Center Press. Order from the Johns Hopkins University Press

American Media: The Wilson Quarterly Reader, edited by Philip S. Cook, Douglas Gomery, and Lawrence W. Lichty (1989).

The Future of News: Television, Newspapers, Wire Services, Newsmagazines, edited by Philip S. Cook, Douglas Gomery, and Lawrence W. Lichty (1992).

Liberty of Expression, edited by Philip S. Cook (1990).

Scholars' Guide to Washington, D.C., for Film and Video Collections, by Bonnie G. Rowan (1980).

Occasional Papers
Available from the Media Studies Project, Woodrow Wilson Center, 370 L'Enfant Promenade, S.W., Ste. 704, Washington, D.C. 20024-2518

#1 *Three Mile Island + 10,* by William Lanouette. Comments by Cass Peterson, Joseph Foucard, and Carol Goldstein. March 1989.

#2 *Foreign Correspondents in Washington,* by Patrick Brogan. April 1989.

#3 *'The First Casualty'—Covering Central America,* by Bryna Brennan. April 1989.

#4 *Covering Israel,* by Milan Kubic. May 1989.

#5 *Moynihan to Moyers: The Black Family and the Political Agenda,* by Howard Husock. September 1989.

#6 *The Atom, Politics, and the Press,* by William Lanouette. December 1989.

Blowing Smoke, by Stephen Klaidman. December 1989. (1989 Essay Contest Winner)

#7 *Covering a Revolution: How Glasnost Is Changing the Moscow Beat,* by Gary Lee. January 1990.

#8 *The Voice of the People? Some Opinions on Public Opinion Polls in the U.S. and the U.S.S.R.,* by Gladys Engel Lang and Kurt Lang. May 1990.

Sound Bite News: Television Coverage of Elections, 1968–1988, by Daniel Hallin. December 1990. (1990 Essay Contest Winner)

#9 *When Walls Come Tumbling Down: Coverage of the East German Revolution,* by Peter Ross Range. June 1991.

#10 *Polling the Political Pollsters,* by Gladys Engel Lang and Kurt Lang. July 1991.

Index